Placement Preparation

Placement Preparation

(More than 1000 Questions)

S PARTHASARATHY
MCA, MPhi., PGDBA, PGDPM,
Lecturer in Computer Applications
Department of Computer Science & Engineering
Thiagarajar College of Engineering
Madurai

NEW AGE
MANAGEMENT

An Imprint of

NEW AGE INTERNATIONAL (P) LIMITED, PUBLISHERS
LONDON • NEW DELHI • NAIROBI
Bangalore • Chennai • Cochin • Guwahati • Hyderabad • Kolkata • Lucknow • Mumbai
Visit us at **www.newagepublishers.com**

Published by New Age International (P) Ltd., Publishers
First Edition: 2006
Reprint: 2017

GLOBAL OFFICES

- **New Delhi** NEW AGE INTERNATIONAL (P) LIMITED, PUBLISHERS
7/30 A, Daryaganj, New Delhi-110002, (INDIA)
Tel.: (011) 23253771, 23253472, **Telefax:** 23267437, 43551305
E-mail: contactus@newagepublishers.com • Visit us at www.newagepublishers.com
- **London** NEW AGE INTERNATIONAL (UK) LTD.
27 Old Gloucester Street, London, WC1N 3AX, UK
E-mail: info@newacademicscience.co.uk • Visit us at www.newacademicscience.co.uk
- **Nairobi** NEW AGE GOLDEN (EAST AFRICA) LTD.
Ground Floor, Westlands Arcade, Chiromo Road (Next to Naivas Supermarket)
Westlands, Nairobi, KENYA, **Tel.:** 00-254-713848772, 00-254-725700286
E-mail: kenya@newagepublishers.com

BRANCHES

- **Bangalore** 37/10, 8th Cross (Near Hanuman Temple), Azad Nagar, Chamarajpet, Bangalore- 560 018
Tel.: (080) 26756823, **Telefax:** 26756820, **E-mail: bangalore@newagepublishers.com**
- **Chennai** 26, Damodaran Street, T. Nagar, Chennai-600 017, **Tel.:** (044) 24353401, **Telefax:** 24351463
E-mail: chennai@newagepublishers.com
- **Cochin** CC-39/1016, Carrier Station Road, Ernakulam South, Cochin-682 016, **Tel.:** (0484) 2377303, **Telefax:** 4051304
E-mail: cochin@newagepublishers.com
- **Guwahati** Hemsen Complex, Mohd. Shah Road, Paltan Bazar, Near Starline Hotel, Guwahati-781 008,
Tel.: (0361) 2513881, **Telefax:** 2543669, **E-mail: guwahati@newagepublishers.com**
- **Hyderabad** 105, 1st Floor, Madhiray Kaveri Tower, 3-2-19, Azam Jahi Road, Near Kumar Theater, Nimboliadda Kachiguda, Hyderabad-500 027, **Tel.:** (040) 24652456, **Telefax:** 24652457
E-mail: hyderabad@newagepublishers.com
- **Kolkata** RDB Chambers (Formerly Lotus Cinema) 106A, 1st Floor, S N Banerjee Road, Kolkata-700 014
Tel.: (033) 22273773, **Telefax:** 22275247, **E-mail: kolkata@newagepublishers.com**
- **Lucknow** 16-A, Jopling Road, Lucknow-226 001, **Tel.:** (0522) 2209578, 4045297, **Telefax:** 2204098
E-mail: lucknow@newagepublishers.com
- **Mumbai** 142C, Victor House, Ground Floor, N.M. Joshi Marg, Lower Parel, Mumbai-400 013
Tel.: (022) 24927869, **Telefax:** 24915415, **E-mail: mumbai@newagepublishers.com**
- **New Delhi** 22, Golden House, Daryaganj, New Delhi-110 002, **Tel.:** (011) 23262368, 23262370, **Telefax:** 43551305
E-mail: sales@newagepublishers.com

ISBN: 978-81-224-1891-0

C-16-12-9931

Printed in India at Ajit Printing Press, Delhi.
Typeset at River Edge, Delhi.

NEW AGE INTERNATIONAL (P) LIMITED, PUBLISHERS
7/30 A, Daryaganj, New Delhi-110002
Visit us at **www.newagepublishers.com**
(CIN: U74899DL1966PTC004618)

DEDICATED TO
MY BELOVED MOTHER

Preface

The IT industry is now in boom. Students are getting placed through both off-campus and on-campus recruitment. Recruitment has become a process of rejection rather than selection due to the large output from the institutions all over the country. The recruitment process normally involves the following stages:

Aptitude test → Technical Test → Technical Interview → Personal Interview

Of course, many companies include group discussion also. The areas where the freshers or experienced professionals find it difficult are the second and third stages mentioned above. Though they have mastered many subjects in their graduation/post-graduation, they find it difficult to quickly recapitulate the basics, which is mandatory to clear any technical test/interview. Hence the need for the preparation of a textbook of this type consisting of more than 1000 questions (short answer and objective type) on various hot topics in Computer Science.

This text book is presented as follows. There are totally twelve chapters. The first eleven chapters provide short answer questions in C Programming, C++ Programming, Data Structures & Algorithms, DBMS, RDBMS, DDBMS, Software Engineering, Software Quality and Software Testing, Operating System, Computer Applications, JAVA Programming and Computer Networks. The last chapter provides objective type questions on the various topics discussed earlier. This "Test Yourself" chapter is given to readers to test themselves after completely studying the earlier chapters.

Being the first edition, this book is prepared and presented in such a way that everybody, even a beginner, will find it easy to have a quick glimpse of the various concepts in Computer Science. The reader can make use of the text book to prepare for technical tests and technical interviews conducted by software companies, competitive exams conducted by State Government and the Government of India for the posts of IT officers, Programmers, IT Managers, and Software Engineers, to clear the technical part of the exams like UGC-NET, SLET etc. The book is targetted at the under-graduate and post-graduate students of any branch, those who aspire to enter the field Information Technology. A list of books that helped us to prepare this textbook is given in the Bibliography. Though great care has been taken in editing this book, I would wholeheartedly accept suggestions for improvement offered by the readers. If you have the patience to go through all the questions starting from the first chapter to the last chapter, I am hopeful that the purpose of the book would be served.

My wholehearted thanks and acknowledgements are due in no small measure to Dr. (Mrs.) Radha Thiagarajan, Chairman, Thiagarajar College of Engineering (TCE), Mr. T. Kannan, Vice Chairman and Correspondent, Dr. V. Abhaikumar, Principal, Dr. R. Rajaram, Head of the Department of Computer Science & Engineering, and my colleagues of the TCE, friends and family. I am thankful to Prof. V. Sankarasubramanian, Head of the Department of English, The Madura College, Madurai, for his invaluable comments and suggestions during the preparation of this book. I sincerely acknowledge the support extended by my father, who is the motivating force behind this project. Finally, I am thankful to New Age International (P) Limited, Publishers, New Delhi, for their support and encouragement.

S. PARTHASARATHY

Acronyms and Abbreviations

2PC	Two-Phase Commit Protocol
3PC	Three-Phase Commit Protocol
4GL	4th Generation Language
ALGOL	Algorithmic Language
ANSI	American National Standards Institute
API	Application Programming Interface
ARP	Address Resolution Protocol
ASCII	American Standard Code for Information Interchange
ATL	Active Template Library
ATM	Automatic Teller Machine
ATP	Acceptance Test Procedure
ATR	Acceptance Test Results
AUT	Application Under Test
AWT	Abstract Windowing Toolkit
B2C	Business-to-Consumer
BASIC	Beginners All Purpose Symbolic Instruction Code
BCNF	Boyce-Codd Normal Form
BDK	Bean Development Kit
BIOS	Basic Input Output System
BIT	Binary Digit
BOM	Bill of Material
BPR	Business Process Reengineering
BSC	Binary Symmetric Channel
BVA	Boundary Value Analysis
C2B	Consumer-to-Business
C2C	Consumer-to-Consumer
CAD	Computer Aided Design
CAM	Computer Aided Manufacturing
CASE	Computer Aided Software Engineering

CBD	Component Based Development Model
CBSE	Component Based Software Engineering
CGI	Common Gateway Interface
CMM	Capability Maturity Model
CMMI	Capability Maturity Model Integration
CMOS	Complementary Metal Oxide Semiconductor
CNF	Chomsky Normal Form
COBOL	Common Business Oriented Language
COCOMO	Constructive Cost Model
COM	Component Object Model
COQ	Cost of Quality
CPM	Critical Path Method
CRC	Class Responsibility Collaborator Modeling
CRM	Customer Relationship Management
CSPEC	Control Specification
CSPM	Certified Software Project Manager
CSQA	Certified Software Quality Analyst
CSQE	Certified Software Quality Engineer
CSTE	Certified Software Test Engineer
DBA	Database Administrator
DBMS	Database Management System
DCL	Data Control Language
DDBMS	Distributed Database Management System
DDL	Data Definition Language
DES	Data Encryption Standard
DFA	Deterministic Finite Automata
DFD	Data Flow Diagram
DHTML	Dynamic Hypertext Markup Language
DLL	Dynamic Link Library
DMA	Direct Memory Access
DML	Data Manipulation Language
DNS	Domain Name System
DOM	Document Object Model

DPDA	Deterministic Pushdown Automata
DRE	Defect Removal Efficiency
DSN	Data Source Name
DSQI	Design Structure Quality Index
DSS	Decision Support System
DTL	Diode – Transistor Logic
DVD	Digital Versatile Disk
ECL	Emitter – Coupled Logic
EDI	Electronic Data Interchange
EER	Extended Entity Relation Diagram
EFT	Electronic Funds Transfer
EIA	Enterprise Integration Application
EIS	Executive Information System
EPROM	Erasable Programmable Read Only Memory
ERD	Entity Relation Diagram
ERP	Enterprise Resource Planning
EVA	Earned Value Analysis
FAST	Facilitated Application Specification Technique
FDM	Frequency Division Multiplexing
FTP	File Transfer Protocol
FTR	Formal Technical Review
GIS	Geographical Information System
GNF	Greibach Normal Form
GUI	Graphical User Interface
HTML	Hypertext Markup Language
HTTP	Hypertext Transfer Protocol
IDC	Internet Database Connector
IIS	Internet Information Server
ISDN	Integrated Service Digital Network
ISO	International Organization for Standardization
ISTQB	International Software Testing Qualifications Board Certified
IT	Information Technology
ICMP	Internet Control Message Protocol
JDBC	Java Database Connectivity
JFC	Java Foundation Classes

KPA	Key Process Area
LAN	Local Area Network
LOC	Lines of Code
MAC	Medium Access Control Sublayer
MAN	Metropolitan Area Network
MAR	Memory Address Register
MFC	Microsoft Foundation Classes
MIS	Management Information System
MODEM	Modulator-Demodulator
MPI	Message Passing Interface
MRP	Materials Requirements Planning
MRP-II	Manufacturing Resource Planning
MST	Minimum Spanning Tree
MTBF	Mean Time Between Failure
MTTF	Mean Time to Failure
MTTR	Mean Time to Repair
NP	Non-Deterministic Polynomial
NSP	Network Service Provider
ODBC	Open Database Connectivity
OLAP	On Line Analytical Processing
OLE	Object Linking and Embedding
OOAD	Object Oriented Analysis and Design
OOPS	Object Oriented Programming System
OSI	Open System Interconnection
OSPF	Open Shortest Path First Protocol
PAL	Programmable Array Logic
PCB	Process Control Block
PCMM	People Capability Maturity Model
PDA	Push Down Automata
PDL	Program Design Language
PDT	Partition Description Table
PERT.	Program Evaluation and Review Technique
POP	Point to Point Protocol
POST	Power On Self Test
PRO/SIM	Prototyping and Simulation Tools

PROM	Programmable Read Only Memory
PSP	Personal Software Process
PSPEC	Process Specification
QFD	Quality Function Deployment
QOS	Quality of Service
RAD	Rapid Application Development
RAID	Redundant Arrays of Inexpensive Disks
RAM	Random Access Memory
RARP	Reverse Address Resolution Protocol
RDBMS	Relational Database Management System
RIP	Routing Information Protocol
RIS	Risk Information Sheet
RMMM	Risk Mitigation Monitoring and Management plan
ROM	Read Only Memory
RPC	Remote Procedure Call
SADT	Structured Analysis and Design Technique
SAP	Systems, Applications and Products in Data Processing
SCM	Supply Chain Management
SCM	Software Configuration Management
SDLC	Software Development Lifecycle
SEI	Software Engineering Institute
SGML	Standard Graphic Markup Language
SLIP	Serial Line Internet Protocol
SMS	Short Messaging Service
SPOOL	Simultaneous Peripheral Operations Online
SQA	Software Quality Assurance
SQL	Structured Query Language
SRS	Software Requirements Specification
SSL	Secure Socket Layer
SSPI	Statistical Software Process Improvement
STD	State Transition Diagram
TCL	Transaction Control Language
TCP/IP	Transmission Control Protocol/Internet Protocol
TDM	Time Division Multiplexing
TFTP	Trivial File Transfer Protocol

TM	Turing Machine
TQM	Total Quality Management
TSL	Test Script Language
TSP	Team Software Process
TTL	Transistor – Transistor Logic
UDP	User Datagram Protocol
UML	Unified Modeling Language
URL	Uniform Resource Locator
V&V	Verification & Validation
VAN	Value Added Network
VPN	Virtual Private Network
VRML	Virtual Reality Model Language
WAN	Wide Area Network
WBS	Work Breakdown Structure
WDM	Wavelength Division Multiplexing
WFF	Well-Formed-Formulae
WIDL	Web Interface Definition Language
WML	Wireless Markup Language
WMS	Warehouse Management System
XML	Extensible Markup Language
XSL	Extensible Style Language

Contents

1 C Programming

1. Who developed the **C language?**

   Dennis M.Ritchie in 1972

2. What type of language is **C**?

   Semi-high level language

3. What is **main()?**

   The main() is a special function used by the C system to tell the computer where the program starts.

4. What is the function of the **'newline'** character denoted as \n?

   A newline character instructs the computer to go to the next (new) line.

5. What is the purpose of a comment statement?

   It increases the readability and understandability of the program and helps in debugging and testing.

6. What is size of operator?

   It is a compile time operator and when used with an operand, it returns the number of bytes the operand occupies.

7. How are the characters in C grouped?

   Letters, digits, special characters and white spaces

8. What are **trigraph characters**?

   ANSI C introduces the concept of "trigraph" sequences to provide a way to enter certain characters that are not available on some keyboards.

9. What is a **constant**?

   C constant refers to fixed values that do not change during the execution of a program.

10. How are the constants classified?

    Integer constants, real constants, single character constant, string constant.

11. What is a **variable**?

    A variable is a data name that may be used to store a data value. A variable may take different values at different times during execution.

12. What are the basic data types used in **C**?

    Char, int, float, and double

13. What is a **storage class**?

    Variables in C can have not only data type but also storage class that provides information about their location and visibility. The storage class decides the portion of the program within which the variables are recognized.

14. List the various storage classes in C.

Auto, static, extern and register.

15. What is an **operator**?

An operator is a symbol that tells the computer to perform certain mathematical or logical manipulations. It is used to manipulate data and variables in programs.

16. List the various C operators.

Arithmetic operators, relational operators, logical operators, assignment operators, increment and decrement operators, conditional operators, bitwise operators and special operators.

17. What is **stdio.h**?

It is standard input-output header file. The instruction #include<stdio.h> tells the compiler to search for a file named stdio.h and place its contents at this point in the program.

18. List the various control statements in C.

'if' statement, 'switch' statement, conditional operator statement and 'goto' statement.

19. What is **switch statement**?

'C' has a built-in multiway decision statement known as a switch. It tests the value of a given variable (or expression) against a list of 'case' values and when a match is found, a block of statements associated with that 'case' is executed.

20. What are the program loops available in C?

The 'while' statement, the 'do' statement and the 'for' statement.

21. Give the format of program loops in C.

(*a*)
```
While (test condition)
    {
    body of the loop
    }
```

(*b*)
```
do
{
body of the loop
} while (test condition);
```

(*c*)
```
for (initialization; test condition; increment/decrement)
{
body of the loop
}
```

22. What is the additional feature in 'for' loop?

More than one variable can be initialized at a time in the 'for' statement.

23. What is an **array**? What are its types?

An array is a group of related data items that share a common name. A list of items can give one variable name using only one subscript and such a variable is called a single-subscripted variable or a one-dimensional array.

Two-dimensional arrays are declared as follows:

Type array-name [row-size][column-size];

Multi-dimensional arrays are declared as follows:

Type array-name [p1][p2][p3].....[px];

24. What is a **string**?

A string is an array of characters. Any group of characters defined between double quotation marks is a constant string.

25. List the string-handling function supported by C library.

(*a*) Strcat() is used to concatenate two strings.

(*b*) Strcmp() is used to compare two strings.

(*c*) Strcpy() is used to copy one string over another.

(*d*) Strlen() is used to find the length of a string.

26. How are C functions classified? Give examples.

C functions can be classified as 'library function' and 'user-defined function'. main() is an example of user-defined function and printf, scanf belong to the library functions.

27. List the various categories of C functions.

(*a*) Functions with no arguments and no return values

(*b*) Functions with arguments and return values

(*c*) Functions with arguments and no return values

28. What is **recursion**?

Recursion is a special case where a function calls itself.

29. How can a function return values?

A function may or may not return a value. If it does, it can return only one value.

30. What is **structure** in C?

C supports a constructed data type known as structure, which is a method for packing data of different types.

31. What is **static structure** in C?

A structure must be declared as static if it is to be initialized inside a function.

32. What is **union** in C?

Unions are a concept borrowed from structures and therefore follow the same syntax as structures. In structure each member has its own storage location, whereas all the members of a union use the same location.

33. What is a bit field?

A bit field is a set of adjacent bits whose size can be from 1 to 16 bits in length.

34. What is a **file**? List the basic file operations.

A file is a place on the disk where a group of related data is stored. The basic file operations are naming a file, opening a file, reading data from a file, writing data to a file and closing a file.

35. What are the various high level I/O functions?

fopen(), fclose(), getc(), putc(), fprintf(), fscanf(), getw(), putw(), fseek(), ftell() and rewind().

36. What is a command line argument?

It is a parameter supplied to a program when the program is invoked.

37. What are **argc** and **argv**?

The variable argc is an argument counter that counts the number of arguments on the command line. The variable argv is an argument vector and represents an array of character pointers that points to the command line arguments. The size of this array will be equal to the value of argc.

38. What is **dynamic memory allocation**?

The process of allocating memory at run time is called **dynamic memory allocation.**

39. Name the various memory allocation functions.

malloc(), calloc(), free() and realloc()

40. What is **C preprocessor**?

C preprocessor is a program that processes the source code before it passes through the compiler. It operates under the control of what is known as preprocessor command lines or directives. It is placed in the source program before the main() line.

41. How are the directives classified?

Macro substitution directives, file inclusion directives and compiler control directives.

42. What is macro substitution?

It is a process where an identifier in a program is replaced by a predefined string composed of one or more tokens.

43. List the various preprocessor directives.

#define, #undef, #include, #ifdef, # end if, #ifndef, #if and #else.

44. List the various forms of macro substitution.

Simple macro substitution, argumented macro substitution and nested macro substitution.

45. What is a **pointer**?

Since memory addresses are simply numbers they can be assigned to some variables which can be stored in memory, like any other variable. Such variables that hold memory addresses are called **'pointers'**.

46. How do we declare a pointer variable?

Data type * pointer-name;

47. What is a **null pointer**?

A null pointer is any pointer assigned the integral value zero. A pointer that is guaranteed not to point to a valid object is called a null pointer.

48. What is meant by a **pointer to a pointer**?

A pointer to a pointer is a construct used frequently in sophisticated programs. To declare a pointer to a pointer, precede the variable name with two successive asterisks. Example: int **q; This declares q to be a pointer to a pointer to an int.

49. What is the difference between **#include <filename>** and **#include "filename"**?

If the filename is surrounded by angle brackets, the preprocessor looks in a special place designated by the operating system. If the file is surrounded by double quotes, the preprocessor looks in the directory containing the source file.

50. What is **typedef**?

C language allows us to create our own names for data types with the typedef keyword. They are especially useful for abstracting global types that can be used throughout a program.

51. What are **'break'** and **'continue'** statements?

'Break' prevents program flow from falling through to the next statement. It should be used with caution since it forces program control to jump discontinuously to a new place. 'Continue' statement provides a means for returning to the top of a loop earlier than normal. It is particularly useful when we want to bypass the remainder of the loop for some reason.

52. What is an **infinite loop**?

An infinite loop is a loop that does not contain a terminating condition or a loop in which the terminating condition is never reached.

53. What is **bit-manipulating operator**?

The bit-manipulation operations enable us to access specific bits within an object and to compare the bit sequences of pairs of objects. The operands for all the bit-manipulation operators must be integers.

54. What are **shift operators**?

The two shift operators, << and >>, enable us to shift the bits of an object a specified number of places to the left or the right.

55. What is **masking**?

The bit-manipulation operators are frequently used to implement a programming technique called 'masking' which allows us to access a specific bit or a group of bits.

56. What is **cast operator**?

If enables us to convert a value to a different type.

57. What is meant by **scope** of a variable?

The scope of a variable determines the region over which we can access the variable by name. There are four types of scope: program, file, function and block.

58. What are **nested structures**?

When one of the fields of a structure is itself a structure, it is called a 'nested structure'. Nested structures are common in C programming because they enable us to create data hierarchies.

59. What is **function allusion**?

A function allusion is a declaration of a function that is defined elsewhere, usually in a different source file. The main purpose of the function allusion is to tell the compiler what type of value the function returns.

60. Why are pointers to functions considered important?

Pointers to functions are a powerful tool because they provide an elegant way to call different functions based on the input data.

61. What is a **stream**?

A stream consists of an ordered series of bytes. I/O is performed through 'streams' that are associated with the files or devices.

62. List the standard streams in C.

stdin, stdout and stderr.

63. What does <stdio.h> contain?

(*a*) Prototype declarations for all the I/O functions.

(*b*) Declaration of the FILE structure.

(*c*) Several macro constants.

64. What is **errno** variable?

There is a global variable called 'errno' that is used by a few of the I/O functions to record errors. 'errno' is an integer variable declared in the errno.h header file.

65. What is the difference between a **definition** and the **declaration** of a variable?

Definition is the place where the variable is created or assigned storage whereas declaration refers to places where the nature of the variable is stated but no storage is allocated.

66. Can we use a **switch** statement to switch on strings?

No. The cases in a **switch** must either have integer constants or constant expressions.

67. Is it necessary that the header files should have an **.h extension**?

No. Traditionally, they have been given an .h extension to identify them as something different from the **.c** program files.

68. Are the expressions ***pointer++ and ++*pointer** the same?

No. *pointer++ increments the pointer and not the value pointed by it, whereas the ++*pointer increments the value being pointed to by the pointer.

69. Give the equivalent pointer expression for x[a][b][c][d].

((*(*(x+a)+b)+c)+d)

70. Where do we use pointers?

Some of the important areas are: (*a*) Dynamic memory allocation (*b*) call by reference (*c*) trees, graphs and so on.

71. How many bytes are occupied by near, far and huge pointers?

A near pointer is 2 bytes long and a far pointer and a huge pointer are 4 bytes long.

72. What is the similarity between a structure, union and an enumeration?

All of them let you define new data types.

73. How would you check whether the contents of two structure variables are the same?

If we need to compare two structures, we will have to write our own function to do so which carries out the comparison field by field.

74. What is the difference between a structure and a union?

A union is essentially a structure in which all of the fields overlay each other. We can use only one field at a time. We can also write to one field and read from another.

75. What is the use of bit fields in a structure declaration?

Bit fields are used to save space in structures having several binary flags or other small fields.

PREDICT THE OUTPUT OR ERROR FOR THE FOLLOWING QUESTION NUMBER 76 TO 108

Note : It is assumed that necessary header files are included and compiled using the turbo C/C++ compiler.

76.
```
#define N 100
# define A 2
main()
{
int a; a=A;
while(a<N)
{   printf("%d\n",a);
a*=a;
}
}
```
OUTPUT: __________

77.
```
main()
{
int m=12345;
long n=987654;
printf("%d\n",m);
printf("%10d\n",m);
printf("%010d\n",m);
printf("%-10d\n",m);
printf("%10ld\n",n);
printf("%10ld\n",-n);
}
```
OUTPUT: __________

78.
```
main()
{
extern int k;
k=40;
printf("%d",sizeof(k));
}
```
OUTPUT: __________

79. main()
```
{int b[5]={2,3};
printf ("\n%d%d%d",b[2]b[3]b[4]);
}
```
OUTPUT: __________

80. main()
```
{
char *str1="xyzq";
char strz[]="xyzq";
printf("%d%d%d",sizeof(str1),sizeof(str2),sizeof("xyzq"));
}
```
OUTPUT: __________

81. main()
```
{
char *cptr,c;
void *vptr,v;
c=20;v=0;
cptr=&c;vptr=&v;
printf("%c%v",c,v);
}
```
OUTPUT: __________

82. void main()
```
{static int i=5;
if(--i)
{
main();
printf("%d",i);
}
}
```
OUTPUT: __________

83. main()
```
{   static int b[20];
int j=0;
b[j]=j++;
printf("\n%d%d%d",b[0],b[1],j);
}
```
OUTPUT: __________

84. main()
```
{
int x=3;
x=x++;
printf("%d",x);
}
```
OUTPUT: __________

85.
```
main()
{   int x=2;
printf("\n%d%d",++x,++x);
}
```
OUTPUT: __________

86.
```
main()
{   int i=-3,j=2,k=0,m;
m=++i&&++j||++k;
printf("\n%d%d%d%d",i,j,k,m);
}
```
OUTPUT: __________

87.
```
main()
{   int a=-5, b=-2;
junk(a,&b);
printf("\na=%d b=%d",a,b);
}
junk(int a,int *b)
{
a=a*a;
*b=*b**b;
}
```
OUTPUT: __________

88.
```
main()
{   int x[]={10,20,30,40,50};
int k;
for(k=0;k<5;k++)
{
printf("\n%d",*x);
x++;
}
}
```
OUTPUT: __________

89.
```
main()
{
int n[25];
n[0]=100;n[24]=200;
printf("\n%d%d",*n,*(n+24)+*(n+0));
}
```
OUTPUT: __________

90.
```
f(int x, int y)
{   int x;
x=40;
return x;
}
```
OUTPUT: __________

91.
```
#define ASK prog
main()
{
printf("ASK");
}
```
OUTPUT : __________

92.
```
#define MAX(x,y) (x>y? x:y)
main()
{
int a;
a=max(3+2,2+7);
printf("%d",a);
}
```
OUTPUT : __________

93.
```
int abc(int I)
{
return (I++);
}
main()
{   int I=abc(10),
printf("%d\n",--I);
}
```
OUTPUT: __________

94.
```
main()
{   int a[10];
printf("%d",*a+1-*a+3);
}
```
OUTPUT: __________

95.
```
main()
{   if(strcmp("ask","ask\0"))
printf("strings are not equal\n");
else
printf("strings are equal\n");
}
```
OUTPUT: __________

96.
```
main()
{
int arr[]={0,1,2,3,4);
int *ptr;
for (ptr=arr+4;ptr>=arr;ptr--)
printf("%d",*ptr);
}
```
OUTPUT: __________

97.
```
main()
{  char s[]="abcdefghij!";
printf("\n%d",*(s+strlen(s));
}
```
OUTPUT: __________

98.
```
main()
{  char str[]="abcdefghi";
char *s;
s=&str[6]-6;
while(*s)
printf("%c",*s++);
}
```
OUTPUT: __________

99.
```
#include "alloc.h"
main()
{
struct node   {
int data;
struct node *link;
};
struct node *p,*q;
p=malloc(sizeof(struct node));
q=malloc(sizeof(struct node));
printf("\n%d%d",sizeof(p),sizeof(q));
}
```
OUTPUT: __________

100.
```
void main()
{  int i=10,j=2;
int *ip=&i,*jp=&j;
int k=*ip/*jp;
printf("%d",k);
}
```
OUTPUT: __________

101.
```
struct a
{  int y;
struct a x;
}
```
OUTPUT: __________

102.
```
main()
{  int I=300;
char *ptr=&I;
*++ptr=2;
printf("%d",I);
}
```
OUTPUT: __________

103. main()

```
{
char *p;
p="%d\n";
p++;p++;
printf(p-2,300);
}
```

OUTPUT: __________

104. main()

```
{
char s[ ] ="C is a philosophy of life";
char t[40];
char *ss, *tt;
ss=s;
tt=t;
while(*ss)
*tt++=*ss++;
*tt='\o';
printf("\n%s",t);
}
```

OUTPUT: __________

105. main()

```
{ int arr[12];
printf("\n%d",sizeof(arr));
}
```

OUTPUT: __________

106. main()

```
{ int I=3;
printf("\naddress of I=%u",&I);
printf("\nvalueof I=%u",I);
}
```

OUTPUT: __________

107. main()

```
{ int I=3;
printf("\nAddress of I=%u",&I);
printf("\nvalue of I=%d",I);
printf("\nvalue of I=%d",*(&I));
}
```

OUTPUT: __________

108. How would you declare the following?

(*i*) An Array of three pointers to chars
(*ii*) An Array of three char pointers

ANSWERS FOR QUESTIONS 76 TO 108

76. OUTPUT

```
2
4
16
```

77. OUTPUT

```
12345
       12345
0000012345
12345
      987654
  -987654
```

78. OUTPUT

ERROR in the program as the extern int k is a declaration and not a definition.

79. OUTPUT

0 0 0

80. OUTPUT

2 5 5

81. OUTPUT

Compilation Error, since size of V is not known.

82. OUTPUT

0 0 0 0

83. OUTPUT

0 0 1

84. OUTPUT

4

85. OUTPUT

No error. The output will vary from one compiler to another.

86. OUTPUT

–2 3 0 1

87. OUTPUT

a= -5 b= 4

88. OUTPUT

Error message

89. OUTPUT

100 300

90. OUTPUT

Error, re-declaration of x;

91. OUTPUT

ASK

92. OUTPUT

9

93. OUTPUT

9

94. OUTPUT

4

95. OUTPUT

Strings are equal

96. OUTPUT

4 3 2 1 0

97. OUTPUT

0

98. OUTPUT

abcdefghi

99. OUTPUT

2 2

100. OUTPUT

Compilation error

101. OUTPUT

Error, Improper usage of structure

102. OUTPUT

556

103. OUTPUT

300

104. OUTPUT

C is a philosophy of life.

105. OUTPUT

24

106. OUTPUT

Address of i = 6485

Value of i = 3

107. OUTPUT

Address of i = 6485

Value of i = 3

Value of i = 3

108. OUTPUT

(*i*) Char *ptr[3];

(*ii*) Char *ptr[3];

2 C++ Programming

1. Compare **C and C++ programming.**

   C++ is a superset of C. It adds to the C language the capability to implement OOP (object oriented programming). C is a procedural language and C++ is an object-oriented language.

2. What are the two major components of an object?

   Data and the functions that act on that data.

3. What is a member function in C++?

   A function contained within a class is called a member function.

4. What is **Data hiding**?

   Protecting data from access by unauthorized function is called 'data hiding'.

5. What are the OOPS concepts?

   Encapsulation, Inheritance and Polymorphism.

6. What is **Polymorphism**?

   The ability of a function or operator to act in different ways on different data types is called polymorphism.

7. Name the header file that enables the user to use cout and cin in C++?

   IOSTREAM.H

8. Which operator is related to concatenation of two strings?

   arithmetic operator (+)

9. If we use the small memory model, what library file must be linked to our program to provide standard library functions?

   CS.LIB

10. What is **Encapsulation**?

    It is the mechanism that binds together the code and the data it manipulates, and keeps both safe from outside interference and misuse.

11. What is **Inheritance**?

    It is a process of creating new classes called derived classes from existing or base classes.

12. How does C++ implement Polymorphism?

    Using (*a*) Function overloading (*b*) Operator overloading (*c*) Virtual functions.

13. Distinguish between Object-oriented language and Object-based language.

    Object-based languages support only objects and classes, whereas Object-oriented languages also support features like inheritance and polymorphism. Visual Basic is an Object-based language Whereas Visual C++ is an Object-oriented language.

14. Arrange in order of preference (highest first) the following kinds of operators: logical, unary, arithmetic, assignment, relational, conditional.

(1) Unary (2) Arithmetic (3) Relational (4) Logical (5) Conditional (6) Assignment

15. What is a **structure variable**?

When accessing a structure member, the identifier to the left of the dot operator is called a structure variable.

16. What is the purpose of the **enumerated data type**?

It brings together a group of integers with user-defined names and constant values.

17. What is a **function argument**?

It is a value sent to the function by the calling program.

18. How many values can be returned by a function?

One.

19. What is the scope of global variables with respect to functions?

Global variables can be accessed from any function.

20. What functions can access an automatic variable?

The functions in which an automatic variable is defined.

21. What is the purpose of a **static automatic variable**?

It makes a variable visible to only one function and retains a value when a function is not executing.

22. What is the significance for passing arguments by reference?

To change the original argument.

23. What is the purpose of a class specifier (declaration)?

A class specifier describes how objects of a class will look when they are created.

24. What are **a class and an object**?

A class is a specification for a number of objects. Objects consist of both data and functions that operate on those data.

25. What is a **Constructor**?

It is a member function with the same name as its class, which is executed every time an object of the class is created.

26. What is a **Destructor**?

It is a member function with the same name as its class but preceded by a tilde (~) symbol. It is called when an object is destroyed.

27. Compare **Constructor and Destructor in C++**.

A constructor has no return type but can take arguments. Constructors can be overloaded. A destructor takes no arguments and has no return value.

28. If three objects of a class are defined, how many copies of the class's data items are stored in memory? How many copies of member function?

Three, One.

29. What is the difference between **structures and classes in C++**?

Member functions and data are, by default, public in structure but private in classes.

30. What is **function overloading**?

Defining multiple functions with the same name is called function overloading. These functions must differ in their number, order or types of arguments.

31. What are **Library functions**?

Library functions are a collection of predefined functions. They are stored in '.lib' files that are shipped with the compiler.

32. List the various ways of passing variables to a function.

(*a*) Call by value (*b*) Call by reference

33. What is an **Inline function**?

The function whose code gets inserted, instead of a jump to the function, at the place where there is a function call is known as an "Inline function".

34. What is **operator overloading**?

It gives the capability to the operator to work on different types of operands.

35. List the access specifiers in C++.

There are three access specifiers in C++ namely Public, Private and Protected.

36. What are **Public, Private and Protected**?

Public data members or member functions can be accessed from anywhere, within the class or from outside the class. Private data members cannot be accessed from outside the class. They can only be accessed within the class. The protected members of the base class are accessible only to the derived classes.

37. Compare the following two statements:
example ex( ); example el(10,200);

The first statement is creating an object ex using a zero-argument constructor. It can also be interpreted as a prototype of function ex( ) whose return type is example. The second statement is creating an object using a two-argument constructor.

38. What is a **dangling pointer**?

Suppose we allocate a chunk of memory and store its address in a pointer. If this chunk of memory is freed and if the pointer continues to point to that location, the pointer is said to be a **dangling pointer**.

39. How do we create a **this** pointer?

The 'this' pointer gets created when a member function (non-static) of a class is called.

40. What is the outcome when we call the constructor explicitly?

Whenever the constructor is called explicitly a nameless object gets created.

41. How do we create an object dynamically?

The keyword **'new'** allows us to create an object dynamically.

42. Can constructors return a value? How does it handle error values?

An error value can never be returned from a constructor. An exception alone can be thrown from within the constructor. Constructor is called whenever an object gets created. There can be no situation where we want to return a value at the time of creation of an object.

43. How do we **overload constructors and destructors**?

Destructors cannot be overloaded. Constructors can be overloaded, as it is like other member functions of the class. But it will not return any value.

44. Show the usage of a **scope resolution operator**.

Void	length	::	addlength	(length L1,	length L2)
1	2	3	4	5	6

1- Return type 2- Name of class of which function is a member
3- Scope resolution operator 4- Function name 5,6 – Function arguments

45. Name some operators which cannot be overloaded?

(*a*) Member access or dot operator **(.)** (*b*) Scope resolution operator **(::)**
(*c*) Conditional operator **(?:)** (*d*) Pointer-to-member operator **(.*)**

46. What is the purpose of **operator overloading**?

It makes C++ operators work with objects and gives new meanings to existing C++ operators.

47. What will happen when you overload an arithmetic assignment operator?

It goes in the object to the left of the operator.

48. What is **multiple inheritance**?

A class that can be derived from more than one base class is called a multiple inheritance.

49. What is the significance of using Inheritance?

Inheritance permits the reusability of software; derived classes can extend the capabilities of base classes with no need to modify or even access the source code of the base class.

50. How will you sort many large objects or structures?

Place pointers to them in an array and sort the array.

51. What is an **Abstract class**?

It is often defined as one that will not be used to create any objects, but exists only to act as a base class of other classes.

52. What is a **friend function**?

A friend can access a class private data, even though it is not a member function of the class.

53. What is a **static function**?

A static function is one that operates on the class in general rather than on objects of the class. It can operate on static variables.

54. Why is assignment operator overloaded?

This is necessary when it must do more than merely coping one object's contents into another.

55. What is a **pure virtual function**?

It is a virtual function that has no body and is used in a base class.

56. Write a statement that a member function can use to return the entire object of which it is a member, without creating any temporary objects.

return *this;

57. Compare the operations of the assignment operator and that of the copy constructor.

They are similar, except that the copy constructor creates a new object. They are different except that they both create a new object.

58. Does the expression delete P delete the pointer or the object being pointed to by P?

The expression delete P deletes the object being pointed to by P.

59. Is it necessary to accept a reference in the **copy constructor**?

It is essential, because if in the copy constructor an object is accepted by value then the copy constructor will fall in a recursive loop.

60. Give an example of pure virtual function?

A Pure virtual function is a virtual function with the expression = 0 added to the declaration.

Example : Class example

```
{ Public :
 virtual void ex ( ) = 0;
};
```

The function ex ( ) is known as a pure virtual function.

61. Compare **static binding and dynamic binding**.

When a function call gets resolved at compile-time it is called static binding or early binding. When the call gets resolved at runtime it is called dynamic binding or late binding.

62. What is a **stream**?

It is used to represent the flow of data. For different kinds of data, different streams are used.

63. Name the three parts of an **iostream system**.

A buffer, a specification system and a translation system.

64. Compare **manipulator and setf( )** function.

The I/O specification class (ios) is at the root of the iostream class hierarchy. Manipulators are the instructions to the output stream to modify the output in various ways. The setf( ) function is used to set the flags of the ios but manipulators directly insert the formatting instructions into the stream.

65. List the three stream classes that are commonly used for disk I/O.

ifstream, ofstream and fstream. They are used for input from file, output to file and both input & output respectively. These classes are declared in 'fstream.h'

66. Compare **iterator and iteration**.

An iterator is an object that moves through the container accessing each element in the container. The process of moving from element to element in the container is called 'iteration'.

67. What is **friend class**?

It is a class where all the member functions and data members of the class become 'friends'.

68. How do we get the information about the object at runtime?

Using typeid( ) operator and dynamic_cast operator.

69. What is the base class for most stream classes?

ios.

70. Define what current position means when applied to files.

The byte location at which the next read or write operation will take place.

71. What is **class library**?

A group of related classes, supplied as a separate product, is often called a class library.

72. What are **templates**?

By using templates, we can design a single class/function that operates on many data types, instead of having to create a separate class/function for each type. When used with functions they are known as 'function templates', whereas when used with classes they are called 'class templates'.

73. How do we return an error value from the constructor?

We cannot return any error value from the constructor, as the constructor doesn't have any return type. However, by throwing an exception we can pass value to 'catch' block.

74. When is a **class template instantiated**?

A **class template** is instantiated by defining an object using the template arguments.

75. What is the size of an object of an empty class?

One byte.

PREDICT THE OUTPUT/ERRORS FOR THE FOLLOWING QUESTION NUMBER : 76 TO 90

76.
```
main()
{
char str[] = "abcdef"
             "xyz";
cout<<str;
}
```
OUTPUT: __________

77.
```
void main()
{
   int j;
for ( j=0;j<11;++j)
cout<<j*j<<" " ;
}
```
OUTPUT: __________

78.
```
void main()
{
 for (int j=0;j<80;j++)
char ch=(j%8) ? ' ' : 'x';
cout<<ch;
}
}
```
OUTPUT: __________

79.
```
const int DAYS = 7;
const int MAX = 10;
void main()
{  char star [DAYS][MAX] = { "sun","mon","tue","wed","thur","fri","sat"};
for (int j=0;j<DAYS;j++)
cout<<star[j]<<endl;
}
```
OUTPUT: __________

80.
```
const int size = 5;
void print (int *ptr)
{
cout<<ptr[0];
}
void print(int ptr[size])
{
cout<<ptr[0];
}
main()
{
int a[size]= { 1,2,,3,4,5};
int *b=new int(size);
print(a);
print(b);
}
```
OUTPUT: __________

81.
```
main()
{
int a,*pa,&ra;
```

```
pa=&a;  ra=a;
cout<<"a="<<a<<"*pa="<<*pa<<"ra="<<ra;
}
```

OUTPUT: __________

82.
```
void main()
{
for(int I=1;I<=10;I++)
cout<<I<<endl;
cout<<I;
}
```

OUTPUT: __________

83.
```
void main()
{   char *x="hai";
    char *y=x;
    cout<<x<<endl<<y;
    y="example";
    cout<<endl<<x<<endl<<y;
}
```

OUTPUT: __________

84.
```
void main()
{   int a=5;int &j=a; int x=10;
    j=x;
    cout<<endl<<a<<endl<<j;
    x=20;
    cout<<endl<<a<<endl<<j;
}
```

OUTPUT: __________

85.
```
const int x=12;
void main()
{   const int *example();
    int *y;
    y=example();
}
const int *example()
{   return (&x);
}
```

OUTPUT: __________

86.
```
void eg(int x, int y);
void main()
{   eg();
}
void eg(int x=0,int y=0)
{   cout<<x<<endl<<y;
}
```

OUTPUT: __________

87.
```
class control
{   public:
    control()
    {   calculate();
        cout<<endl<<"abcd";
    }
void calculate()
{   display();
    cout<<endl<<"xyz";
}
void display()
{   cout<<endl<<"pqr";
}
};
void main()
{
control c1;
}
```
OUTPUT: __________

88.
```
class a
{   int j;
}
main()
{
    //statements
}
```
OUTPUT: __________

89.
```
void main()
{   char str[]="example";
    char *p="examination";
    cout<<endl<<str;
    cout<<endl<<p;
    cout<<endl<<(void *)str;
    cout<<endl<<(void *) p;
}
```
OUTPUT: __________

90.
```
class sample
{   public:
    sample()
    {               }
    sample (sample &s)
    {     cout<<"copy constructor"<<endl;
    }
sample fun(sample s)
    {
```

```
sample t;
t=s;
return t;
}
};
void main()
{
sample s1,s2,s3;
s3=s1.fun(s2);
}
```

OUTPUT: __________

ANSWERS FOR QUESTIONS 76 TO 90

76. OUTPUT:

abcdefxyz

77. OUTPUT:

0 1 4 9 16 25 36 49 64 81 100

78. OUTPUT:

x x x x x x x x x

79. OUTPUT:

Sun
Mon
Tue
Wed
Thurs
Fri
Sat

80. OUTPUT:

Compilation Error: function 'void print (int *)' already has a body.

81. OUTPUT:

Compiler Error: 'ra', reference must be initialized.

82. Output

Displays 1 to 11 each in a new line.

83. OUTPUT:

hai
hai
hai
example

84. OUTPUT:
10
10
10
10

85. OUTPUT:

Compilation error due to type mismatch.

86. OUTPUT:
Error

87. OUTPUT:
pqr
xyz
abcd

88. OUTPUT:

No error class a is considered as return type of main().

89. OUTPUT:
example
examination
0x8fa20fea
0x8f55oo11

90. OUTPUT:
Copy constructor
Copy constructor

3 Software Engineering

1. What is **Software Engineering**?

   Software engineering is a discipline that integrates process, methods and tools for the development of computer software.

2. What are the layers in software engineering?

   Tools, Methods, Process and Quality focus.

3. What is **KPA** in software engineering?

   The foundation for software engineering is the process layer. Process defines a framework for a set of key process areas (KPA) that must be established for effective delivery of the software engineering technology.

4. List the umbrella activities in software engineering.

   Software project tracking and control, formal technical reviews, document preparation and production, reusability management, measurement, risk management, software quality assurance and software configuration management.

5. List the various software engineering models.

   Linear sequential model, prototyping model, RAD (Rapid Application Development) model, evolutionary software process models, component-based development model, formal methods model.

6. What is **RAD**?

   It is an incremental software development process model that emphasizes an extremely short development cycle.

7. List the various evolutionary software process models.

   The incremental model, the spiral model, the WINWIN spiral model, the concurrent development model.

8. What is a **spiral model**?

   This model was proposed by Boehm. It is an evolutionary software process model that couples the iterative nature of prototyping with the controlled and systematic aspects of the linear sequential model.

9. What is a **task region**?

   A spiral model is divided into a number of framework activities called task regions.

10. What is a **WINWIN spiral model**?

    This model defines a set of negotiation activities at the beginning of each pass around the spiral. The objective of this activity is to elicit project requirements from the customer.

11. What is a **CBD model**?

    The component based development (CBD) model incorporates many of the characteristics of the spiral model. It is evolutionary in nature, demanding an iterative approach to the creation of software.

12. What is the **formal method model**?

    It encompasses a set of activities that lead to the formal mathematical specification of computer software. Formal methods enable a software engineer to specify, develop and verify a computer-based system by applying a rigorous, mathematical notation.

13. What is **software project management**?

    It is an umbrella activity within software engineering. It begins before any technical activity is initiated and continues throughout the definition, development and support of computer software.

14. Name the factors influencing software project management.

    People, Product and Process.

15. Define the term "software metric".

    It refers to a broad range of measurements for computer software. Measurements can be applied to the software process with the intent of improving it on a continuous basis. Software metrics are analyzed and assessed by software managers. Measures are often collected by software engineers.

16. What is **PSP**?

    The Personal software process (PSP) is a structured set of process descriptions, measurements, and methods that can help engineers to improve their personal performance.

17. What is **SSPI**?

    SSPI (Statistical Software Process Improvement) uses software failure analysis to collect information about all errors and defects encountered as an application, system or product is developed and used.

18. What is the difference between **direct and indirect software measures**?

    Direct measures of the software engineering process include cost and effort applied. Direct measures of the product include lines of code (LOC) produced, execution speed, memory size and defects reported over some set period of time. Indirect measures of the product include functionality, quality, complexity, efficiency, reliability and maintainability.

19. What are the indicators of **software quality**?

    Correctness, maintainability, integrity and usability of software are the indicators of software quality.

20. How can the **integrity** of a system be defined?

    Integrity = summation [(1-threat) x (1-security)] where threat and security are summed over each type of attack.

21. What is **DRE**?

DRE (Defect Removal Efficiency) is a measure of the filtering ability of quality assurance and control activities as they are applied throughout all process framework activities. DRE = E/(E+D) where E is the number of errors found before delivery of the software to the end-user and D is the number of defects found after delivery.

22. What is **software project planning**?

The objective of software project planning is to provide a framework that enables the manager to make reasonable estimates of resources, cost and schedule.

23. What is meant by **software scope**?

The first activity in software project planning is the determination of software scope. It describes the data and control to be processed, function, performance, constraints, interfaces and reliability.

24. What are the resources influencing software project?

People, reusable software components, hardware/software tools.

25. What is the **empirical estimation model**?

An estimation model for computer software uses empirically derived formula to predict effort as a function of LOC or FP. A typical estimation model is derived using regression analysis on data collected from past software projects.

26. What is the **COCOMO model**?

The COCOMO (Constructive Cost Model) is a hierarchy of estimation models that address the application composition model, the early design stage model and the post-architecture stage model. Three different sizing options available here are object points, function points and lines of source code.

27. What is **software equation**?

It is a dynamic multivariable model that assumes a specific distribution of effort over the life of a software development project.

28. What is meant by **outsourcing**?

It is a concept where the software engineering activities are contracted to a third party who does the work at lower cost and hopefully provides higher quality.

29. What are **Risk Analysis** and **Management**?

Risk analysis and management are a series of steps that help a software team to understand and manage uncertainty. Everyone involved in the software process participate in risk analysis and management.

30. What **types of risks** are we likely to encounter as the software is built?

Project risks, Technical risks, Business risks.

31. What is meant by **Risk Identification**?

Risk identification is a systematic attempt to specify threats to the project plan. One method for identifying risks is to create a risk item checklist.

32. What is **Risk Projection**?

Risk projection, also called risk estimation, attempts to rate each risk in two ways: the likelihood or probability that the risk is real and the consequences of the problems associated with the risk, should it occur.

33. What is a **Risk table**?

A Risk table provides a project manager with a simple technique for risk projection.

34. What is **software safety and hazard analysis**?

Software safety and hazard analysis are software quality assurance activities that focus on the identification and assessment of potential hazards that may affect software negatively and cause an entire system to fail.

35. What is **RMMM** plan?

The RMMM (Risk Mitigation Monitoring and Management plan) documents all the work performed as part of risk analysis and is used by the project manager as part of the overall project plan.

36. What is **RIS**?

Each risk is documented individually using a risk information sheet (RIS). In most cases, the RIS is maintained using a database system.

37. What is **software project scheduling**?

It is an activity that distributes the estimated effort across the planned project duration by allocating the efforts to specific software engineering tasks.

38. List the number of basic principles that guide software project scheduling.

Compartmentalization, Interdependency, time allocation, effort validation, defined responsibilities, defined outcomes and defined milestones are the basic principles guiding software project scheduling.

39. What are the two project scheduling methods that can be applied to software development?

(*a*) **PERT** (Program Evaluation and Review Technique) (*b*) **CPM** (Critical Path Method)

40. What is an **earned value system**?

A technique for performing the quantitative analysis of progress does exist. It is called earned value analysis **(EVA)**. The earned value system provides a common value scale for every software project task, regardless of the type of work being performed. The total hours to do the whole project are estimated, and every task is given an earned value based on its estimated percentage of the total.

41. What is **software configuration management**?

SCM (Software Configuration Management) is an umbrella activity that is applied throughout the software process. SCM is developed to identify change, to control change, to ensure that change is being properly implemented and to report changes to others who may be interested.

42. Why is SCM so important?

It is an important element of software quality assurance. Its primary responsibility is the control of change.

43. What is **version control**?

Version control combines procedures and tools to manage different versions of configuration objects that are created during the software process.

44. What is **software configuration audit**?

It complements the formal technical review by assessing a configuration object for characteristics that are generally not considered during review.

45. What is **System engineering**?

Software engineering occurs as a consequence of a process called **system engineering.** Instead of concentrating solely on software, system engineering focuses on a variety of elements, analyzing, designing and organizing those elements into a system that can be a product, a service or a technology for the transformation of information or control.

46. What is **Business process engineering**?

The system engineering process is called business process engineering when the context of the engineering work focuses on a business enterprise.

47. What is **Product engineering**?

When a product is to be built, the process is called product engineering. Both business process engineering and product engineering attempt to bring order to the development of computer-based systems.

48. What is **Software requirements analysis**?

It is a process of discovery, refinement, modeling and specification.

49. What is **Requirements analysis**?

It is a software engineering task that bridges the gap between system level requirements engineering and software design.

50. What are the various phases in software requirement analysis?

(*a*) Problem recognition (*b*) Evaluation & synthesis (*c*) Modeling (*d*) Specification
(*e*) Review

51. What is **FAST**?

FAST (Facilitated Application Specification Technique) encourages the creation of a joint team of customers and developers who work together to identify the problem, propose elements of the solution, negotiate different approaches and specify a preliminary set of solution requirements.

52. What is **QFD**?

QFD (Quality Function Deployment) is a quality management technique that translates the needs of the customer into technical requirements for software. QFD identifies three types of requirements: (*i*) Normal requirements (*ii*) Expected requirements (*iii*) Exciting requirements.

53. What types of models do we create during requirements analysis?

Functional models and Behavioral models.

54. What is **Prototyping**?

Prototyping offers an alternative approach to the requirements gathering phase that results in an executable model of the software from which requirements can be refined.

55. What are the primary objectives of an **analysis model**?

(*a*) To describe what the customer requires.

(*b*) To establish a basis for the creation of a software design.

(*c*) To define a set of requirements that can be validated once the software is built.

56. What are the **elements** of the analysis model?

(*a*) Entity relationship diagram (*b*) Data flow diagram (*c*) State-transition diagram and (*d*) At the core of the model lies the data dictionary.

57. What is **Cardinality**?

Cardinality is the specification of the number of occurrences of one [object] that can be related to the number of occurrences of another [object].

58. What is **Modality**?

The modality of a relationship is 0 if there is no explicit need for the relationship to occur or the relationship is optional. The modality is 1 if an occurrence of the relationship is mandatory.

59. What are **Control specification (CSPEC) and Process specification (PSPEC)**?

CSPEC represents the behavior of the system. PSPEC is used to describe all flow model processes that appear at the final level of refinement.

60. What is **Data dictionary**?

It is an organized listing of all data elements that are pertinent to the system, with precise, rigorous definitions so that both user and system analyst will have a common understanding of inputs, outputs, components of stores and intermediate calculations.

61. What are **Cohesion and Coupling**?

Cohesion is a qualitative indication of the degree to which a module focuses on just one thing. Coupling is a measure of the relative interdependence among modules. Cohesion is a measure of the relative functional strength of a module.

62. What is **Software architecture**?

Software architecture provides a holisting view of the system to be built. It depicts the structure and organization of software components, their properties, and the connections between them.

63. What is **Architectural design**?

It represents the structure of data and program components that are required to build a computer-based system.

64. What is **User interface design**?

It creates an effective communication medium between a human and a computer. User interface design begins with the identification of user, task and environmental requirements.

65. When will **Component-level design** take place?

Component-level design, also called procedural design, occurs after data, architectural and interface designs have been established.

66. How is **software reliability** measured?

It is measured in terms of mean time between failures (MTBF).

67. Has the **software crisis** been overcome?

No, not yet. One of the main reasons for the software crisis is the lack of thrust for software testing. Test engineers can contribute significantly to the software quality.

68. What is **CASE** and who does it?

CASE (Computer-Aided Software Engineering) tools assist software engineering managers and practitioners in every activity associated with the software process. Project mangers and software engineers use CASE.

4 Software Quality and Software Testing

1. What is **SQA**?

   SQA (Software Quality Assurance) is an umbrella activity that is applied throughout the software process.

2. What are **Quality of design and Quality of conformance**?

   Quality of design refers to the characteristics that designers specify for an item. Quality of conformance is the degree to which the design specifications are followed during manufacturing. The greater the degree of conformance, the higher the level of quality of conformance.

3. What is **Software quality control**?

   Quality control involves the series of inspections, reviews and tests used throught the software process to ensure each work product meets the requirements placed upon it.

4. What is **Quality assurance**?

   Quality assurance consists of the auditing and reporting functions of management. It will ensure that product quality meets its goals.

5. What are the components of cost of quality?

   Cost of quality includes all costs incurred in the pursuit of quality or in performing quality-related activities. Quality cost may be divided into costs associated with prevention, appraisal and failure.

6. How do we define **Software quality**?

   Software quality is defined as conformance to explicitly stated functional and performance requirements, explicitly documented development standards, and implicit characteristics that are expected of all professionally developed software.

7. What is the role of an **SQA group**?

   (*a*) Prepares an SQA plan for a project.

   (*b*) Participates in the development of the project's software process description.

   (*c*) Reviews software engineering activities to verify compliance with the defined software process.

   (*d*) Audit designated software work products.

   (*e*) Ensures that deviation in software work and work products is documented and handled according to a documented procedure.

   (*f*) Records any noncompliance and reports to senior management.

8. What is **FTR**?

   FTR (Formal technical review) is a software quality assurance activity performed by software engineers. The primary objectives of FTR are: (*a*) To uncover errors in function, logic, or implementation for any representation of the software (*b*) To verify that the software under review meets its requirements.

9. What is **statistical software quality assurance**?

It reflects a growing trend throughout industry to become more quantitative about quality. It is carried out through information about software defects, using the Pareto principle and tracing each defect to its underlying cause.

10. What is **software reliability**?

It is defined in statistical terms as "the probability of failure free operation of a computer program in a specified environment for a specified time".

11. What is **MTBF**?

MTBF = MTTF + MTTR

MTBF = Mean – time between failures.

MTTF = Mean – time to failure

MTTR = Mean – time to repair.

12. What is **software availability**?

It is the probability that a program is operating according to requirements at a given point in time and is defined as

Availability = [MTTF / (MTTF + MTTR)] * 100%

13. What is **software safety**?

It is a software quality assurance activity that focuses on the identification and assessment of potential hazards that may affect software negatively and cause an entire system to fail.

14. What is **ISO 9001 standard**?

It is the quality assurance standard that applies to software engineering. The standard contains 20 requirements that must be present for an effective quality assurance system.

15. Why is software quality assurance important?

It is the mapping of the managerial precepts and design disciplines of quality assurance onto the applicable managerial and technological space of software engineering.

16. Name some **software quality metrics.**

(*i*) Number of defects found per KDSI (known as defect density)

(*ii*) Number of changes requested by the customer after the software is delivered.

(*iii*) MTBF (Mean time between failures) *i.e.* the average time between failures.

(*iv*) MTTR (Mean time to repair) *i.e.* the average time required to remove a defect after it is detected.

17., Compare **Product Quality Metrics and Process Quality Metrics.**

The product quality metrics are different from the process quality metrics. The product quality metrics reflect the quality of the product whereas the process quality metrics reflect how well the process is defined.

18. What is **CMM**?

CMM (Capability Maturity Model) is a model developed by the software engineering institute to grade software development organizations based on their process maturity.

19. What is **software process maturity**?

The extent to which a process is explicitly defined, managed, measured, controlled and effective is defined as software process maturity.

20. What are the **levels in CMM**?

An organization is given one of the 5 grades or levels as level 1 to level 5.

Level 1 organization does not follow any processes to develop software. They do everything on ad hoc basis. Level 5 organizations have very mature processes and continuously improve their processes to improve product quality. However, CMM levels indicate only the process quality and not product quality.

21. Compare **TQM and CMM.**

CMM addresses the management of quality of software aspects of the project *i.e.* CMM is confined to software quality management of the organization whereas TQM (Total quality management) addresses both hardware and software quality management.

22. What is **CMMI**?

The Capability maturity model integration (CMMI) for software engineering is the result of the SEI's efforts to develop an integrated improvement framework for the following standards for quality system management:

(*i*) CMM for software (SW – CMM)

(*ii*) EIA / IS 731

(*iii*) IPD – CMM VO.98

There are two representations of CMMI framework namely staged and continuous.

23. Why is **PSP** required?

The **SEI (Software Engineering Institute)** developed the personal software process (PSP) which defines the processes to be followed by individuals. The philosophy of PSP is simple: plan year work, track your work and analyze your work so that you will continuously improve yourself.

24. What is **PCMM level**?

The people capability maturity model (PCMM) was developed at the SEI to measure and improve the human resources development practices. Organizations are graded from level 1 to level 5 to measure the effectiveness of human resources development practices.

25. What is **software testing**?

It is a critical element of software quality assurance and represents the ultimate review of specification, design and code generation.

26. Who does the software testing?

During early stages of testing, a software engineer performs all tests. However, as the testing process progresses, testing specialists may become involved.

27. What are the attributes of a **good** test?

(*a*) A good test has a high probability of finding an error.

(*b*) A good test is not redundant.

(*c*) A good test should be **the best of breed.**

(*d*) A good test should be neither too simple nor too complex.

28. What are **Black–Box testing and White–Box testing?**

White–box testing, sometimes called **glass–box testing** is a test case design method that uses the control structure of the procedural design to derive the test cases. Black–box testing, also called **behavioral testing,** focuses on the functional requirements of the software.

29. What is **Basis path testing?**

It is a white–box testing technique first proposed by McCabe. It enables the test case designer to derive a logical complexity measure of a procedural design and use this measure as a guide for defining a basis set of execution paths.

30. How is basis path testing carried out?

Using representations like flow graph, graph matrix and software metrics like cyclomatic complexity and control structure testing.

31. What is **control structure testing?**

The control structure testing completely scans all the logical conditions, data flow and loops through condition testing, data flow testing and loop testing.

32. What are **Condition testing and Data flow testing?**

Condition testing is a test case design method that exercises the logical conditions contained in a program module. The data flow testing method selects test paths of a program according to the locations of definitions and uses of variables in the program.

33. What is **loop testing?**

It is a white-box testing technique that focuses exclusively on the validity of loop constructs. Four different classes of loops can be defined simple loops, concatenated loops, nested loops and unstructured loops.

34. What is **equivalence partitioning?**

It is a black-box testing method that divides the input domain of a program into classes of data from which test cases can be derived.

35. What is **boundary value analysis?**

Values that are on the boundary of equivalence classes are high field test cases. Example: for (I=0;I<=50;I++) { statements }. In this code, I=50 is a boundary value. It is a test case design technique that complements equivalence partitioning.

36. What is **orthogonal array testing?**

It can be applied to problems in which the input domain is relatively small but too large to accommodate exhaustive testing. The orthogonal array testing method is particularly useful in finding errors associated with region faults--an error category associated with a faulty logic within a software component.

37. What are **verification and validation**?

Verification refers to the set of activities that ensure that software correctly implements a specific function. Validation refers to a different set of activities that ensure that the software that has been built is traceable to customer requirements.

38. What is the overall strategy for software testing?

Four types of testing are conducted to the software product. Unit testing begins first and concentrates on each unit of the software as implemented in source code. Then comes integration testing, where focus is on design and the construction of the software architecture. Next is validation testing, where requirements established as part of software requirements analysis are validated against software. Finally comes the system testing where the software and other system elements are tested as a whole.

39. When are we done with software testing?

There is no definitive answer to this question. We can never say that testing is over; the burden simply shifts from the software engineer to the customer. Every time the user executes the computer program, the program is being tested.

40. What are the **two levels in integration testing**?

Top-down integration and bottom-up integration.

41. What is **regression testing**?

In the context of an integration test strategy regression testing is the re-execution of some subset of tests that has already been conducted to ensure that changes have not propagated unintended side effects.

42. What is **smoke testing**?

It is an integration testing approach that is commonly used when "shrink wrapped" software products are being developed.

43. What is **Alpha and Beta testing**?

The alpha test is conducted at the developer's site by a customer. The beta test is conducted at one or more customer sites by the end-user of the software.

44. What is **system testing**?

It is actually a series of different tests whose primary purpose is to fully exercise the computer based system. Types of system tests include (1) Recovery testing (2) Security testing (3) Stress testing and (4) Performance testing.

45. What is **Debugging**?

Debugging is the process that results in the removal of the error. It is not testing but always occurs as a consequence of testing.

46. What is **Mutation testing**?

Mutation testing is required to ensure that the software does not fail. It is also a good debugging mechanism. After the software works correctly, mutation testing can be done to simulate wrong inputs.

47. What is **WinRunner**?

It is a very powerful automated testing tool for functional/regression testing. Using WinRunner, we can record GUI operations. While recording, WinRunner automatically creates a test script. This test script can be run automatically later on for carrying out unattended testing.

48. What is **TSL**?

Test Script Language (TSL) is a scripting language with syntax similar to C language. There are four categories of TSL functions. They are:

(*a*) Analog functions
(*b*) Context sensitive functions
(*c*) Customization functions
(*d*) Standard functions

49. What are the features of the WinRunner application?

(*a*) Synchronization of test cases
(*b*) Data driven testing
(*c*) Rapid testing
(*d*) GUI check points

50. What is **Data driven testing**?

Data driven testing simplifies the testing process as we can just generate one test case with constants, and then replace these constants with variables. This type of testing is very important for most database applications.

51. What is **SilkTest**?

To facilitate unattended testing, silktest has an in-built customizable recovery system. It can be used for testing a variety of applications such as VB, standalone JAVA, websites, databases, etc.

52. What are the components of Silktest?

It has two components that execute as separate processes: (*a*) Host software (*b*) Agent software. Host software is the component that is used to develop test plans and test scripts. The agent software is the component that interacts with the GUI of our application.

53. What are the steps in silk test testing process?

(1) Creating a test plan (2) Recording a test frame (3) Creating test cases (4) Running test cases and interpreting these results.

54. What is **LoadRunner**?

The Mercury Interactive's LoadRunner is used to test the client/server applications such as database management systems and websites. Using LoadRunner, with minimal infrastructure and manpower, performance testing can be carried out. LoadRunner simulates multiple transactions from the same machine and hence it creates a scenario of simultaneous access to the application. Hence instead of 'real' users, 'virtual' users are simulated.

55. What is an **Apache JMeter**?

It is an open source testing tool used to test the performance of the application when it is under heavy load. It can be used to test both static and non-static data. It puts a heavy load on the server, tests the performance and analyzes the results when many users access the application simultaneously.

56. What is **Test Director**?

Test engineers need to study the requirements of the software in detail. The requirements define what needs to be tested. Hence an SRS document gives the testing objectives. The TestDirector provides the features of linking the tests with the requirements. It can be integrated with other tools such as WinRunner and LoadRunner. Hence, the test scripts generated using these tools can be incorporated in the test plan.

57. List the non-functional requirement of a software product.

Reliability, portability, usability, efficiency, delivery, time, and safety requirements etc.

58. What is **open source software**?

It is a revolutionary concept in software development. The source code is freely distributed by the author, and it can be redistributed without any license fee.

59. What is **software process**?

The step-by-step procedure to convert a problem definition into a working software product. This procedure is divided into different stages such as requirements engineering design, coding, testing and maintenance.

60. Does every software project need testing?

While all projects will benefit from testing, some projects may not require independent test staff to succeed. The answer depends on the size and context of the project, the risks, the development methodology, the skill and experience of the developers, and other factors.

61. Why does software have bugs?

Bugs are normally found in software because of software complexity, programming errors, changing requirements and poor scheduling of software projects.

62. What is a **walkthrough**?

A **walkthrough** is an informal meeting for evaluation or informational purposes. Little or no preparation is usually required.

63. What is an **inspection**?

An **inspection** is more formalized than a **walkthrough**, typically with 3-8 people including a moderator, a reader and a recorder to take notes.

64. What are the common problems in the software development process?

Poor requirements, unrealistic schedule, inadequate testing, walkthroughs and inspections.

65. What is **good code**?

A **good code** is a code that works, is bug free and is readable and maintainable.

66. What makes a good software test engineer?

A good test engineer has a 'test to break' attitude, an ability to take the point of view of the customer and a strong desire for quality.

67. What makes a good **software quality assurance engineer**?

The same qualities a good tester has are useful for a quality assurance engineer. Additionally, software quality assurance engineer must be able to understand the entire software development process and how it can fit into the business approach and goals of the organization.

68. What is a **test plan**?

A software project test plan is a document that describes the objectives, scope, approach and focus of a software testing effort. The process of preparing a test plan is a useful way to think through the efforts needed to validate the acceptability of a software product.

69. What is a **test case**?

A test case is a document that describes an input, action, or event and an expected response, to determine whether an application is working correctly.

70. How will you carryout software testing when you don't have enough time?

One way is to use risk analysis to determine where testing should be focused.

71. What is **Extreme Programming**?

Extreme Programming (XP) is a software development approach for small teams on risk-prone projects with unstable requirements.

72. Will automated testing tools make testing easier?

For small projects, the time needed to learn and implement the automated testing tools may not be worthier unless the testing team is already familiar with the tools. For larger projects, or on-going long-term projects, these tools can be of high value.

73. Name some **certifications** for software quality assurance and test engineers.

CSQE (Certified Software Quality Engineer) program, **CSQA** (Certified Software Quality Analyst), **CSTE** (Certified Software Test Engineer) and **CSPM** (Certified Software Project Manager) certifications, **ISTQB** (International Software Testing Qualifications Board) certified tester.

5 Data Structures and Algorithms

1. What is an **algorithm**?

   It is any well-defined computational procedure that takes some value, or set of values, as input and produces some value, or set of values, as output.

2. What is a **data structure**?

   A data structure is a way to store and organize data in order to facilitate access and modifications.

3. What is **probabilistic analysis**?

   It is the method of using probability to analyze problems. We use probabilistic analysis to analyze the running time of an algorithm.

4. What is a **randomized algorithm**?

   We call an algorithm randomized if its behavior is determined not only by its input but also by values produced by a random-number generator.

5. What is **heap data structure**?

   The (binary) heap data structure is an array object that can be viewed as a nearly complete binary tree. Each node of the tree corresponds to an element of the array that stores the value in the node.

6. What is a **priority queue**?

   A priority queue is a data structure for maintaining a set of elements, each with an associated value called a key.

7. What is **counting sort**?

   Counting sort assumes that each of the n input elements is an integer in the range 0 to k for some integer k, when k = O(n), the sort runs in O(n) time.

8. What is **bucket sort?**

   Bucket sort runs in linear time when the input is drawn from a uniform distribution. Bucket sort is fast because it assumes something about the input.

9. Name some elementary data structures.

   Stacks, Queues

10. What are **stacks and queues?**

    Stacks and queues are dynamic sets in which the element removed from the set by the DELETE operation is pre-specified. In a stack, the policy is LIFO (Last-in, First-out). In a queue, the policy is FIFO (First-in, First-out).

11. What is a **linked list**?

    A linked list is a data structure in which the objects are arranged in a linear order.

12. What is a **binary tree**?

A binary tree T is a structure defined on a finite set of nodes that either contains no nodes, or is composed of three disjoined sets of nodes: a root node, a binary tree called its left subtree, and a binary tree called its right subtree.

13. What is a **null tree**?

The binary tree that contains no nodes is called the empty tree or null tree.

14. What is a **full binary tree**?

It is a binary tree where each node is either a leaf or has degree exactly 2.

15. What is **K-ary tree**?

It is a positional tree in which for every node, all children with labels greater than k are missing. Thus, a binary tree is a k-ary tree with k=2. A complete k-ary tree is a k-ary tree in which all leaves have the same depth and all internal nodes have degree k.

16. What is a **hash table**?

A hash table is an effective data structure for implementing dictionaries. The expected time to search for an element in a hash table is O(1). A hash table is a generalization of the simple notion of an ordinary array.

17. What are **collision and chaining**?

A collision is a situation where the two keys may hash to the same slot. In chaining, we put all the elements that hash to the same slot in a linked list. The dictionary operations on a hash table T are easy to implement when collisions are resolved by chaining.

18. What makes a good hash function?

A good hash function satisfies the assumption of simple uniform hashing; each key is equally likely to hash to any of the m slots, independently of where any other key has hashed to.

19. What is **universal hashing**?

Universal hashing is a technique of choosing the hash function randomly in a way that is independent of the keys that are actually going to be stored.

20. What is **open addressing**?

In open addressing, all elements are stored in the hash table itself. Each table entry contains either an element of the dynamic set or nil.

21. What is **linear probing**?

Given an ordinary hash function h':U→ {0,1,2,...m–1} which we refer to as an auxiliary hash function, the method of linear probing uses the hash function h(k,I)=(h′(k)+I) mod m for I=0,1,2,....m–1. Given key k, the first slot probed is T [h′(k)], i.e. the slot given by the auxiliary hash function. We next probe slot t[h'(k)+1] , and so on up to slot T[m-1].

22. What is **double hashing**?

It is one of the best methods available for open addressing because the permutations produced have many of the characteristics of randomly chosen permutations. Double hashing uses a hash function of the form h(k,I)=(h1(k)+Ih2(k)) mod m, where h1 and h2 are auxiliary hash functions.

23. What is a **binary search tree**?

It is a binary tree where in addition to a key field and satellite data, each node contains fields left, right and p that point to the nodes corresponding to its left child, its right child and its parent, respectively. If a child or the parent is missing, the appropriate field contains the value NIL. The root node is the only node in the tree whose parent field is NIL.

24. What is the property of a binary-search tree?

Let x be a node in a binary search tree. If y is a node on the left subtree of x, then key[y] ≤ key[x]. If y is a node in the right subtree of x, then key[x] ≤ key[y].

25. What is a **red black tree**?

A red black tree is a binary search tree with one extra bit of storage per node. Its color can be either RED or BLACK.

26. When is a binary search tree called a red-black tree?

A binary search tree is a red black tree if it satisfies the following red-black properties: (1) Every node is either red or black. (2) The root is black (3) Every leaf (NIL) is black. (4) If a node is red, then both its children are black. (5) For each node, all paths from the node to descendant leave contain the same number of black nodes.

27. What is an **AVL tree**?

An AVL tree is a binary search tree that is height balanced: for each node x, the heights of the left and right subtrees of x differ by atmost 1. To implement an AVL tree, we maintain an extra field in each node: h[x] is the height of node x.

28. What is a **treap**?

It is a binary search tree with a modified way of ordering the nodes. Each node x in the tree has a key value—key [x]. In addition, we assign priority [x], which is a random number chosen independently for each node. All priorities are distinct and also all keys are distinct.

29. What is an **order-statistic tree T**?

It is simply a red-black tree with additional information stored in each node.

30. How do we augment a **data structure**?

Augmenting a data structure can be broken into four steps:

(*a*) Choosing an underlying data structure;

(*b*) Determining additional information to be maintained in the underlying data structure;

(*c*) Verifying that the additional information can be maintained for the basic modifying operations on the underlying data structure; and

(*d*) Developing new operations.

31. How is **dynamic programming** algorithm generated?

The development of a dynamic programming algorithm can be broken into a sequence of four steps:-

(*a*) Characterizing the structure of an optimal solution;

(*b*) Recursively defining the value of an optimal solution;

(*c*) Computing the value of an optimal solution in a bottom-up fashion; and

(*d*) Constructing an optimal solution from computed information.

32. What is an **optimal binary search tree**?

For a given set of probabilities, our goal is to construct a binary search tree whose expected search cost is smallest. We call such a tree an optimal binary search tree.

33. What is a **Greedy algorithm**?

A greedy algorithm always makes the choice that looks best at the moment. That is, it makes a locally optimal choice in the hope that this choice will lead to a globally optimal solution. Greedy algorithms do not always yield optimal solutions, but for many problems they do.

34. What are **Huffman codes**?

Huffman codes are a widely used and very effective technique for compressing data. Huffman's greedy algorithm uses a table of the frequencies of occurrence of the characters to build up an optimal way of representing each character as a binary string.

35. How will you construct a Huffman code?

Huffman invented a greedy algorithm that constructs an optimal prefix code called a Huffman code.

36. What is **amortized analysis**?

In an amortized analysis, the time required to perform a sequence of data structure operations is averaged over all the operations performed. It can be used to show that the average cost of an operation is small, if one averages over a sequence of operations, even though a single operation within the sequence might be expensive.

37. What is a **B-tree**?

B-trees are balanced search trees designed to work on magnetic disks or other direct-access secondary storage devices. B-trees are similar to red-black trees but they are better at minimizing disk I/O operations.

38. Define the **height of a B-tree**.

The number of disk accesses required for most operations on a B-tree is proportional to the height of the B-tree.

39. What is a **binomial tree**?

It is an ordered tree defined recursively. For the binomial tree B_k, there are 2^k nodes. The height of the tree is k, there are exactly kc_i nodes at depth i for i=0,1,....k and the root has degree k, which is greater than that of any other node.

40. What is a **binomial heap H**?

It is a set of binomial trees that satisfies the following binomial heap properties.

(*a*) Each binomial tree in H obeys the min-heap property.

(*b*) For any non-negative integer k, there is atmost one binomial tree H whose root has degree k.

41. What is a **Fibonacci Heap**?

It is a collection of min-heap ordered trees. The trees in a Fibonacci heap are not constrained to be binomial trees. Unlike trees within binomial heaps which are ordered, the trees within Fibonacci heaps are rooted but unordered.

42. What is a **topological sort**?

A topological sort of a directed acyclic graph G = (V,E) is a linear ordering of all its vertices such that if G contains an edge (u,v) then u appears before v in the ordering.

43. State the **zero-one principle.**

It says that if a sorting network works correctly when each input is drawn from the set {0,1}, then it works correctly on arbitrary input numbers.

44. What is a **sorting network**?

A sorting network is a comparison network for which the output sequence monotonically increases for every input sequence.

45. What is **NP-Completeness**?

A language $L \subseteq \{0,1\}^*$ is NP-complete if 1) $L \in NP$ and 2) $L' \leq pL$ for every $L' \in NP$. If a language L satisfies property 2, but not necessarily property 1, we say that L is NP-hard.

46. Give an example of NP-complete.

A clique in an undirected graph G=(V,E) is a subset $V' \subseteq V$ of vertices, each pair of which is connected by an edge in E. A clique is a complete subgraph of G. The size of a clique is the number of vertices it contains. The clique problem is NP-Complete.

47. What is a **spanning tree**?

A spanning tree is a tree associated with a network. All the nodes of the graph appear on the tree once. **MST (Minimal Spanning Tree)** is a spanning tree organized so that the total edge weight between nodes is minimized.

48. What are the methods to find MST?

(*a*) Prim's algorithm: O(n*n) and (*b*) Kruskal's algorithm: O(e*log e)

49. What is a **bottleneck-spanning tree T**?

A bottleneck-spanning tree T of an undirected graph G is a spanning tree of G whose largest edge weight is minimum over all spanning trees of G.

50. Name the **collision resolution techniques.**

(*a*) Open addressing (closed hashing). Here, the method used is overflow blocks.

(*b*) Closed addressing (open hashing). Here, the method used includes linked lists, binary tree, etc.

6 Computer Applications

1. Name some applications of computer science which enable an organization to improve its performance.

   ERP packages, MIS, DSS, SCM, BPR, EIS and OLAP.

2. **Expand the following:** ERP, MIS, DSS, SCM, BPR, EIS, OLAP, MRP, MRPII, EDP, CRM, TQM and EDIFACT

   ERP – Enterprise Resource Planning
   MIS – Management information system
   DSS – Decision support system
   SCM – Supply chain management
   BPR – Business process reengineering
   EIS – Executive information system
   OLAP – On line analytical processing
   MRP – Materials requirements planning
   MRP II – Manufacturing resource planning
   EDP – Electronic data processing
   CRM – Customer relationship management
   TQM – Total quality management
   EDIFACT – Electronic data interchange for administration, commerce and transport.

3. What is **ERP**?

   ERP covers the techniques and concepts employed for the integrated management of businesses as a whole, from the view point of the effective use of management resources, to improve the efficiency of an enterprise. ERP packages are integrated software packages that support these ERP concepts.

4. What are the advantages of ERP?

   Business integration, flexibility, standardization, better planning and ability to make use of the latest technology.

5. What is a **Business model**?

   A Business model is a representation of the actual business--what the various business functions of the organization are, how they related are, what their interdependencies are and so on.

6. What is **Data Mining**?

   It is the process of identifying valid, novel, potentially useful and ultimately comprehensible information from databases that are used to make crucial business decisions.

7. What is a **Data Warehouse**?

   It is a database designed to support decision making in an organization. It is updated batch-wise and is structured for fast online queries and summaries for managers.

8. Why is **OLAP** required?

   It is used for applications such as product profitability and piecing analysis, activity based costing, manpower planning and quality analysis.

9. What is **supply chain management**?

   It is a process of managing the facilities and distribution options that perform the function of procurement of materials, transformation of these materials into intermediate and finished products and distribution of these finished products to customers.

10. What is **BPR**?

    Dr. Michael Hammer defined Business Process Reengineering as the fundamental rethinking and radical redesign of business processes to achieve dramatic improvements in critical, contemporary measures of performance such as cost, quality, service and speed.

11. What are the techniques used in Data mining?

    Neural networks, rube induction, evolutionary programming, case based reasoning (CBR), decision trees, genetic algorithms and nonlinear regression methods.

12. What is the **evolution of ERP**?

    MRP → MRP II → ERP → SCM

13. What are the three approaches in ERP implementation?

    There are three different approaches to ERP implementation. They are:

    (*i*) The 'big bang' approach
    (*ii*) Location-wise approach
    (*iii*) Module-wise approach

14. What are the three ways of evaluating ERP software?

    The evaluation of ERP software can be done in three perspectives namely organizational, business and technological perspective.

15. What are the **business modules** in an ERP package?

    Financial management, HR Management, Manufacturing, Production planning, Plant maintenance, Materials management and Quality management.

16. What are the two versions of the **SAP ERP package**?

    SAP (systems, applications and products in data processing) is the leading global provider of client/server business application solution. SAP ERP package comes in two versions: the mainframe version (SAP R/2) and the client/server version (SAP R/3).

17. Name some **ERP vendors.**

    SAP, Baan, JD Edwards, Ramco system and Oracle Corporation.

18. What is **EIA**?

    Enterprise Integration Application (EIA) products promise to speed the work of linking applications and eliminating or reducing the need to develop a custom code.

19. What is **BOM**?

    Bill of material (BOM) defines the relationship of components to end items.

20. What is **CAD/CAM?**

CAD (Computer–Aided Design) / CAM (Computer-Assisted Manufacturing) systems are computer programs or integrated packages for workstation hardware and software that allow the user to draw and easily modify product designs on a computer screen. CAD–engineered designs are converted automatically into software programs for computerized production machines.

21. What is **MIS?**

Management information system (MIS) is a computer-based system that optimizes the collection, collation, transfer and presentation of information throughout an organization through an integrated structure of databases and information flow.

22. What is **DSS?**

A DSS (Decision support system) is an information and planning system that provides the ability to interrogate computers on ad-hoc basis, analyze information and predict the impact of decisions before they are made.

23. What is **EIS?**

An EIS (Executive Information System) is an information system that consolidates and summarizes the ongoing transactions within an organization.

24. What is **E-Commerce?**

Electronic commerce (E-commerce) means doing business online or selling and buying products and services through web.

25. What is **EDI?**

EDI (Electronic Data Interchange) is the electronic communication of transactions between organizations such as orders, confirmations and invoices.

26. What is **TQM?**

TQM (Total Quality Management) is both a philosophy and a set of guiding principles that represent the foundation of a continuously improving organization. It is a strategic, integrated management system for achieving customer satisfaction.

27. What is **WMS?**

WMS (Warehouse Management System) is a software that integrates mechanical and human activities with an information system to effectively manage warehouse business processes and direct warehouse activities.

28. Name the four basic phases in ERP implementation.

(*a*) Defining the problem (*b*) Defining solutions (*c*) Getting down to work (*d*) Going live.

29. What are the advantages of a **Data warehouse?**

(1) Less expensive (2) Better enterprise intelligence (3) Enhanced customer service (4) Business reengineering (5) Effective decision making (6) Increased operational and production databases.

30. What are the major components of a Data warehouse?

(*i*) Summarized data (*ii*) Operational systems of record (*iii*) Architecture of Data warehouse (*iv*) Archives.

31. What is **CRM**?

Customer Relationship Management (CRM) is to add value for customers through those processes that involve direct contact with customer before, during and after sales.

32. Compare **CAD and CAM**.

CAD systems are interactive computer graphics systems used for product design. The CAD technology significantly reduces the time required for product design, and provides tremendous flexibility in design. CAM software integrates the operations of all computers-controlled machines. CAM can have on-line and off-line applications.

33. How is computer network related to E-Commerce?

E-Commerce is an emerging concept that describes the process of buying and selling or exchanging of products, services and information via computer networks including the internet.

34. What are the applications of **Extranets**?

Enhanced communication, productivity enhancement, business enhancement, cost reduction and information delivery.

35. What is **embedded extranet?**

One site connected to the Internet has an embedded extranet of another company so that the company at the back can provide information to the customers seamlessly.

36. What is **B2B**?

Business-to-Business EC (B2B) is an electronic trading where both the buyers and the sellers are organizations.

37. What is **B2C**?

Business-to-Consumer EC is a situation where a business is selling online to an individual consumer.

38. What is **e-cash**?

Electronic Cash (e-cash) is the cash in an electronic form, usually stored on a smart card and/or in software called digital wallet.

39. What is an **Intelligent Agent**?

Intelligent Agents and their subset software agents are computer programs that help the users to conduct routine tasks, search and retrieve information, support decision making and act as domain experts. Agents are used to support many tasks in Electronic Commerce.

40. What is **C2C (Consumer-to-Consumer)**?

In this category consumer sells directly to consumers. Examples are individuals selling in classified ads and selling residential property, cars, and so on.

41. What is **C2B (Consumer-to-Business)**?

This category includes individuals who sell products or services to organizations, as well as individuals who seek sellers, interact with them, and conclude a transaction.

42. Name some commercial web servers that help E-Commerce.

The three servers that are more popular are: (*i*) Apache server (*ii*) Microsoft's Internet Information Server (IIS) and (*iii*) Netscape's Enterprise Server.

43. What are the **major legal issues related to EC**?

Major issues include privacy, protecting intellectual property, controlling internet indecency, preventing fraud, establishing a tax framework, controlling gambling, determining jurisdiction and protecting both sellers and buyers.

44. What are **Biometric controls**?

Biometric controls provide access procedures that match every valid user with a unique user identifier (UID). They also provide an authentication method to verify that users requesting access to the computer system are really those whom they claim to be.

45. What is **DES**?

Data encryption standard (DES) is a published federal encryption standard created to protect unclassified computer data and communications.

46. What is **SWOT** analysis?

SWOT is an acronym used to describe particular strengths, weaknesses, opportunities and threats for a company.

47. List the **applications of extranets**.

Enhanced communication, productivity enhancement, business enhancements, costs reduction and information delivery.

48. What is the relationship among the Internet, Intranet and Extranet?

The Internet is a public and global network open to anybody. An Intranet is a corporate network whose access is protected by firewalls. An Extranet is an extended intranet, which links the remote intranets, or individuals, over the virtual private network built on the internet.

49. What is **Electronic Banking**?

Electronic banking, also known as **cyberbanking**, virtual banking, home banking, and online banking, includes various banking activities conducted from home, business, or on the road, instead of at a physical bank location.

50. What are the changes brought by E-Commerce?

Everything will be changed, starting with marketing theories and practices and concluding with product innovation and supply chain management.

7 JAVA Programming

1. What type of language is **JAVA**?

   Java is an object-oriented, multi-threaded programming language developed by Sun Microsystems in 1991. In Java development environment there are two parts: a Java compiler and a Java interpreter. The compiler generates bytecode instead of machine code and the interpreter executes the Java program.

2. What is the disadvantage of **bytecode**?

   Execution speed.

3. List some features of JAVA.

   Secured, portable, object-oriented, robust, multithreaded and dynamic.

4. What is a **Swing**?

   It is a set of user interface components that is implemented entirely in java.

5. What are the three **different kinds of variables** in Java?

   Instance variables, Local variables and Class variables. Local variables are used inside blocks as counters or in methods as temporary variables. Once the block or the method is executed, the variable ceases to exist. Instance variables are used to define attributes or the state of a particular object. Class variables are global to a class and to all the instances of the class.

6. What is meant by **Literals**?

   A Literal represents a value of a certain type where the type describes the behavior of the value. There are different types of literals. They are *(a)* Number *(b)* Character *(c)* Boolean *(d)* String

7. What are **wrapper classes**?

   Wrapper classes are provided for the primitive data types in order to use theses types as objects.

8. What is a **class**?

   A class defines the shape and behavior of an object and is a template for multiple objects with similar features.

9. What is the purpose of **this** keyword?

   The 'this' keyword is used inside any instance method to refer to the current object. The value of 'this' refers to the object on which the current method has been called.

10. What is a **method**?

    Methods are functions that operate on instances of classes in which they are defined. Objects can communicate with each other using methods and can call methods in other classes.

11. What are the various levels of access control? What is the difference between them?

    Access control is the process of controlling visibility of a variable or method. There are four levels of visibility that are used. They are Public, Private, Protected and Package.

12. What are **constructors and finalizer**?

    A constructor method is a special kind of method that determines how an object is initialized when created. They have the same name as the class and do not have any return type. The finalizer method functions in contradiction to the constructor method. Finalizers are called just before the object is garbage collected and its memory is reclaimed. The Finalizer method is represented by finalize().

13. What is an **inner class**?

    An inner class is a nested class whose instance exists within an instance of its enclosing class and has direct access to the instance members of its enclosing instance.

14. What is **garbage collection**?

    In Java, deallocation happens automatically. The technique that accomplishes this is called **garbage collection**.

15. List some **string methods** used in Java.

    Length( ), CharAt( ), equals( ), CompareTo( ), Concat( ), Substring( ), replace( ), toLowercase( ), toUppercase( ), trim( ), valueof( ).

16. What is **String Buffer**?

    String Buffer is a peer class of string that provides much of the common use functionality of strings. Strings represent fixed-length character sequences.

17. Name some demerits of Java.

    Java does not support multidimensional arrays and operator overloading. However, an array of arrays can be created.

18. What is an **interface**?

    An interface is a collection of abstract behavior specifications that individual classes can implement.

19. What is a **package**?

    Packages in Java are a way of grouping together related classes and interfaces.

20. What is **overriding**?

    Overriding is the creation of a method in the subclass that has the same signature (i.e.) name, number and type of arguments, as a method in the super class. This new method hides the method of the super class.

21. What is the purpose of keyword **final**?

    The word **final** is used to indicate that no further alterations can be made. Classes can be declared as **final** indicating that the value of that particular variable cannot be changed.

22. What is an **abstract class**?

    Abstract classes are classes from which instances are usually not created. It is basically used to contain common characteristics of its derived classes.

23. What are the advantages of **inheritance**?

(*i*) Reusability of code (*ii*) Data and methods of a super class are physically available to its subclasses.

24. What is an **exception**?

An exception is an abnormal condition, which arises during the execution of a program. Java handles exceptions using five keywords – try, catch, finally, throws and throw.

25. What are the merits of a package?

Packages contain a set of classes in order to ensure that its class names are unique. Packages are containers for classes that are used to compartmentalize the class name space.

26. List the various **exceptions** available in Java.

ArrayIndexoutofBoundsException, EOFException, FileNotFoundException, IOException, InterruptedIOException, InvalidClassException, NegativeArraySizeException, NumberFormatException, SQLException and UnknownHostException.

27. How are **file operations** carried out in Java?

File I/O operations are performed using methods found in a class file found in java.io.package. Three types of constructors are found in the file class.

28. What are the methods available with the InputStream/ Reader class?

read( ), skip( ), available( ), close( ), mark( ) and reset( ).

29. What are the two types of **file streams** available in Java?

File stream comprises of the FileInputStream and FileOutputStream. The FileInputStream class helps in reading data from the actual disk files. The FileOutputStream class helps to create a file and write data into it using the methods under OutputStreamClass.

30. What is **Random Access File Class**?

It can be used for both input and output to a single file. Although it is not a stream class, it provides the same platform – independent formatting methods as the DataStream classes.

31. What is **AWT**?

The **Abstract Windowing Toolkit (AWT)** is an API (Application Programming Interface) that is responsible for building the graphical user interface (GUI). It is a part of the Java Foundation Classes (JFC). The java.awt package contains all classes for creating user interface and for painting graphics and images.

32. How are Java programs classified?

Java programming is classified into two groups namely applications and applets. An applet is a dynamic and interactive program that can run inside a web page displayed by a Java – capable browser such as Hot Java or Netscape.

33. What are the restrictions associated with applets?

(1) Applets cannot read or write to the file system.

(2) Applets cannot run any programs on the system.

(3) Applets cannot communicate with any server other than the one in which they were stored originally.

34. Name some of the tags used inside an applet.html file?

<Applet>, </Applet>, CODE, CODEBASE, WIDTH and HEIGHT.

35. How will you pass parameters to an **applet**?

Parameters can be passed to an applet by using the PARAM tag, which has two attributes NAME and VALUE.

36. What are the main methods of the applet class?

The main methods of Applet class are init( ), start( ), stop( ), destroy( ), paint( ) and repaint( ).

37. What is a **thread**?

Thread is a line of execution. In a single threaded system there is only one execution line.

38. What is an **event**?

When an event is fired, it is received by one or more listeners that act on that event. Components can handle events by themselves or can delegate it to objects called listeners.

39. What is an **EventListener**?

An EventListener interface typically has a separate method for each distinct event type the event class represents. There are two types of mouse event listeners – MouseListener and MouseMotionListener.

40. What is a **Panel**?

The Panel is a recursively nestable container often used to divide the screen space into a number of cells.

41. What is **layout manager class**?

The iayout manager classes are a set of classes that implement the java.Awt.Layout manager interfaces and help to position the components in a container.

42. What are the basic layout managers?

FlowLayout, BorderLayout, GridLayout, GridBagLayout, and CardLayout.

43. What is a **frame class**?

The frame class is used to create standard application windows independent of the browser that contains the applet.

44. How do we build and manage **menus** in Java?

Java's AWT provides three classes MenuBar, Menu and MenuItem to build and manage menus.

45. What is **JFC**?

Java Foundation Class (JFC) is an extension for AWT. It consists of five major packages namely swing, pluggable look and feel, drag and drop, accessibility, and 2D.

46. Give the **syntax** of an **interface**.

An interface is a collection of abstract behavior that individual classes can implement. It is defined like a class.

Syntax:

```
<access>          <interface Name>{
<return Type>   <method Name 1>   (<parameter. List>);
        .
        .
        .
    <type>        <variable Name 1> = <value>;
        .
        .
                    }
```

Here the access is either public or without specification.

47. What is **multithreading**?

A process containing multiple threads to execute its different sections is called multithreading. There are four states associated with a thread—namely new, runnable, blocked and dead.

48. What are the **interfaces** of java. lang?

Cloneable, Comparable and Runnable.

49. What is **JDBC**?

JDBC (Java Database Connectivity) is a software layer that allows developers to write real client–server projects in Java. It was designed to be a very compact, simple interface focusing on the execution of raw SQL statements and retrieving the results.

50. What are the **components of JDBC**?

Application, Driver Manager and Driver.

51. What is **JDBC API**?

It defines a set of interface and classes to be used for communicating with a database. These interface and classes are found in the java.sqlpackage.

52. What is the purpose of the **super** keyword?

The **super** keyword allows a subclass to refer to its immediate super class.

53. What is the usage of **repaint( )** method?

This method is used in case an applet is to be repainted.

54. What is a **Dot operator**?

It is used to obtain the value of the instance variable. The general form for accessing instance variables using the dot operator is given below:

<Object Reference>. <Variable Name> Where <Object Reference> is the name of the object and <Variable Name> is the instance Variable.

55. What is a **new operator**?

The **new** operator creates a single instance of a named class and returns a reference to that object.

PREDICT THE OUTPUT OR ERROR FOR THE FOLLOWING QUESTION NUMBER 56 TO 80

56.
```
Class one {
Public static void main (String args[]){
for (int i=0;i<8;i++){
for (int j=0;j<i;j++){
System.out.print (" "+(i*j));
}}}
```
OUTPUT:______________

57.
```
Class two {
Public static void main (String args[]){
float C; float f = 69;
C= (f-32)*5/9;
System.out.println ("Centrigrade equivalent is" + C + "C");
}}
```
OUTPUT:______________

58.
```
Class sample {
Public static void main (String args[]){
int r = 5, C;
While(r<=1){
C=1;
While(C<=5){
System.out.println (r%2==1?"*":"#");
++C;
}
--r;
System.out.println ();
}}}
```
OUTPUT:______________

59.
```
Class argu {
Public static void main (String args[]){
for (int i=0; i<agrs.length;i++){
System.out.println ("Arg "+i+":"+args[i]);
}}}
```
OUTPUT:______________

60.
```
Public class sub {
static int a[] = {2,6,5,9};
Public static void main(String args[]){
for (int i=0;i<a.length;i++)
{System.out.println ("Subscript is" + String.Valueof(i)+"Value is"+String.valueof(a[i]));
}}}
```
OUTPUT:______________

61. Class first {
Public static void main (String args[]) {
System.out.println ("WELCOME");
}}
OUTPUT:______________

62. Class sec {
Public static void main (String args[]) {
x=90; short y=40; float z=10.99f;
System.out.println ("Integer x is" +x);
System.out.println ("Short y is" +y);
System.out.println ("Float z is" + z);
}}
OUTPUT:______________

63. Class count {
Public static void main (String args[]) {
int a=1; int b=2; int c=++b;
int d=a++;
c++;
System.out.println ("a= "+a);
System.out.println ("b= " +b);
System.out.println ("c= "+c);
System.out.println ("d= "+d);
}}
OUTPUT:______________

64. Class bits {
Public static void main (String args[]) {
int a=1; int b=2; int c=3;
a=a | 4;
b>>=1;
c<<=1;
a=a^c;
System.out.println ("a= "+a);
System.out.println ("b= "+b);
System.out.println ("c= "+c);
}}
OUTPUT:______________

65. Class demo{
Public static void main (String args[]) {
for (int j=0;j<10;j++){
System.out.print (+j+" ");
if(j%2==0)
continue;
System.out.println (" ");
}}}
OUTPUT:______________

66. Class pr {

```
Private int x=10;
void var(){
System.out.println ("value is "+x);
}
Public static void main (String args[]){
Priv p1 = new Priv();
System.out.println ("Value is "+p1.x);
p1.var();
}}
```

OUTPUT:______________

67. Class demo {

```
Public static void main (String args[]) {
String s1 = "Hellosir";
String s2 = "Hellosir";
String s3 = "Thankyou";
String s4 = "HELLO";
System.out.println (s1.equals(s2));
System.out.println (s1.equals(s3));
System.out.println (s1.equals(s4));
}}
```

OUTPUT:______________

68. Class throwexception {

```
Public static void main (String args[]) throws ArithmeticException {
System.out.println ("inside main");
int i=0;
int j=400/i;
System.out.println ("this statement");
}}
```

OUTPUT:______________

69. Class Def {

```
Public static void main (String args[]) {
int i[]={2};
i[10]=20;
}}
```

OUTPUT:______________

70. import java.awt.*;

```
import java.applet.*;
Public class clip {
Public void paint (Graphics g){
g.clipRect(10,10,150,100);
g.setFont(new Font("TimesRoman",font.ITALIC,28));
g.filloval(100,60,80,80);
g.drawString("Happy",50,30);
}}
```

OUTPUT:______________

71. Public class Fun {
```
int g()
{
System.out.println("inside g");
int n()
{
System.out.println("inside h");
return 1;
}
return 0;
}
Public static void main (String[]  args)
{int c;
c=g();
}}
```
OUTPUT:______________

72. Class te{
```
Public static void main (String args[]) {
{
Button b;
b.setText("Hai");
}}
```
OUTPUT:______________

73. Class t
```
{
Public int eg;
Public static void main (String argv[]) {
int i = new t().eg;
System.out.println(i);
}}
```
OUTPUT:______________

74. Class t
```
{
int s=200;
t()
{
this(s++);
}
t(int i)
{
System.out.println (s);
}
Public static void main (String argv[]) {
new t();
}}
```
OUTPUT:______________

75. Class two

```
{
void two()
{
System.out.println("Sample");
}
Public static void main (String argv[])
{
two ex=new two();
}}
```

OUTPUT:_____________

76. Class stat

```
{
Public static void main (String[] args)
{
int j=getX();
}
Public int getX()
{
return 5;
}}
```

OUTPUT:_____________

77. Class convert

```
{
Public static void main (String args[]) {
String str;
str="50";
int j=Integer.valueof(str).intvalue();
System.out.println(j);
str="50.1";
double d=Double.valueof(str).doublevalue();
System.out.println(d);
}}
```

OUTPUT:_____________

78. Class A

```
{
Public static void main (String[]  args) {
int x[] = {1,2};
int y[] = (int[])x.clone();
System.out.print((x= = y)+" ");
x[1]++;
System.out.println(y[1]);}}
```

OUTPUT:_____________

79. import java.util.StringTokenizer;

```
Class test
{
Public static void main(String args[])
{
String x= "1  2  3  4";
StringTokenizer s= new StringTokenizer(x);
while (s.hasMoreTokens())
System.out.println(s.nextToken());
}}
```

OUTPUT:______________

80. int x=1+(int)(Math.random()*7);

What does this code do?

ANSWERS FOR QUESTIONS 56 TO 80

56. Error: closing brace for the class is missing

57. OUTPUT

Centrigrade equivalent is 20.555555C

58. OUTPUT

```
*****
#####
*****
#####
*****
```

59. OUTPUT

```
Arg   1: 123
Arg   2:This is the 2nd argument
Arg   3:third
Arg   4:fourth
```

60. OUTPUT

```
Subscript is 0 value is 2
Subscript is 1 value is 6
Subscript is 2 value is 5
Subscript is 3 value is 9
```

61. Error: There is no semicolon in 3rd line

62. Error: The variable x is not declared

63. OUTPUT

```
a=2
b=3
c=4
d=1
```

64. OUTPUT

```
a=3
b=1
c=6
```

65. OUTPUT
0 1
2 3
4 5
6 7
8 9

66. Compilation error

67. OUTPUT
true
false
false

68. OUTPUT
inside main
Exception in thread "main" java.lang.ArithmeticException:/by zero at ThrowsException.main(ThrowsException.java:5)

69. Error:

Exception in thread "main"java.lang.ArrayIndexOutofBoundsException:10 at DefException.main(defException.java:4)

70. Error:

The 3rd line should be as follows:

Public class clip extends Applet

71. Compilation error

72. Runtime error: NullPointerException

73. OUTPUT
0

74. Compilation error: Cannot use 'this' inside the constructor

75. Compilation error: 'void' before two()

76. Compilation error: Cannot access a non-static member

77. OUTPUT
50 50.1

78. OUTPUT
false 2

79. OUTPUT
1
2
3
4

80. The code always assigns an integer to variable x in the range between 1 and 7.

8 Operating System

1. What is an **operating system**?

   An operating system is a program that manages the computer hardware. It also provides a basis for application programs and acts as an intermediary between the user of a computer and the computer hardware.

2. What is meant by a **control program**?

   A control program manages the execution of user programs to present errors and improper use of the computer. It is especially concerned with the operation and control of I/O devices.

3. What is meant by **SPOOL**?

   More sophisticated forms of I/O buffering called "Simultaneous Peripheral Operations Online (SPOOL)" use disks to temporarily store input and output of jobs.

4. What is **Multiprogramming**?

   The most important aspect of job scheduling is the ability to carry out multiprogramming. Multiprogramming is an attempt to increase the CPU utilization by always having something for the CPU to execute. Here the CPU will never be idle.

5. What are the types of operating systems (OS)?

   (*a*) Batch OS (*b*) Multiprogramming OS (*c*) Time-sharing OS (*d*) Real-time systems

   (*e*) Combination OS (*f*) Distributed OS.

6. What are the activities of an operating system?

   Each type of operating system possesses the following aspects: (*a*) Processor scheduling (*b*) Memory management (*c*) I/O management (*d*) File management.

7. What is the purpose of **Real-time systems**?

   It is used in an environment where a large number of events, mostly external to the computer system, must be accepted and processed in a short time or within certain deadlines.

8. What is a **distributed operating system**?

   It is a collection of autonomous computer systems capable of communication and cooperation via their hardware and software interconnections. The key objective of a distributed operating system is transparency.

9. Name the different views of an operating system.

   Two types are: (1) command language users (2) System call users.

   Command language users are those who obtain services of the operating system by means of commands, say typed at the terminal or embedded in a batch job. System call users invoke services of the operating system by means of run-time system calls. These are usually embedded in and activated during execution of programs.

10. What is **Multitasking**?

It denotes an operating system that supports concurrent execution of programs on a single processor without necessarily supporting elaborate forms of memory and file management. A multiprogramming operating system is also a multitasking operating system whereas the converse is not implied.

11. What is **Implicit tasking**?

It means that the processes are defined by the system. It is used in general purpose multiprogramming systems such as time-sharing.

12. What is **Explicit tasking**?

This means that programmers explicitly define each process and some of its attributes. It is used in situations where high performance or explicit control of system activities is desired.

13. What are the two fundamental relations among concurrent processes?

(*a*) Competition (*b*) Cooperation

14. What is a **process**?

A process is a program in execution. As a process executes, it changes state. The state of a process is defined by that process's current activity.

15. What are the general categories of **process states**?

(*i*) Dormant (*ii*) Ready (*iii*) Running (*iv*) Suspended

16. What is **PCB**?

The operating system groups all information that it needs about a particular process into a data structure called a PCB (Process Control Block) or process descriptor.

17. What is **Scheduling**?

Scheduling refers to a set of policies and mechanisms built into the operating system that govern the order in which the work to be done by a computer system is completed.

18. What is a **Scheduler**?

A Scheduler is an operating system module that selects the next job to be admitted into the system and the next process to run.

19. Name the **three different types of schedulers**?

(*i*) Long-term scheduler (*ii*) Medium-term scheduler (*iii*) Short-term scheduler.

20. What is **swapping**?

Saving the image of a suspended process in secondary storage is called **Swapping** and the process is said to be swapped out or rolled out.

21. What are the criteria followed by schedulers in their attempt to maximize system performance?

(*i*) Processor utilization (*ii*) Throughput (*iii*) Turnaround time (*iv*) Waiting time (*v*) Response time.

22. What is **throughput?**

It is the number of jobs which are completed per time unit.

23. Define **Turnaround time.**

It is the time that elapses from the moment a program or a job is submitted until it is completed by a system.

24. Define **Waiting time.**

It is the time that a process or a job spends waiting for resource allocation due to contention with others in a multiprogramming system.

25. Define **Response time.**

It is the time that elapses from a moment the last character of a command line launching a program or a transaction is entered until the first result appears on the terminal.

26. Name the various **scheduling algorithms.**

(*a*) FCFS (First-come, First-served) scheduling.

(*b*) STRT (Shortest Remaining Time Next) Scheduling.

(*c*) Preemptive algorithms.

(*d*) Round-Robin algorithms.

27. What are **Multi-level/Multi Queues scheduling?**

A multi-queue scheduling algorithm has been created for a situation in which jobs are easily classified into different groups. A multi-queue scheduling algorithm partitions the ready queue into separate queues.

28. What is **Multi-level Feedback queue?**

Here, jobs are permanently assigned to a queue upon entry to the system. Jobs do not move between queues.

29. What is **interprocess synchronization?**

A set of protocols and mechanisms used to preserve system integrity and consistency when the concurrent processes share resources that are serially reusable.

30. What is a **critical section?**

It is a sequence of instructions with a clearly marked beginning and end. It usually safeguards updating of one or more shared variables. Only the process executing the critical section is allowed to access the shared variable. All other processes should be prevented from doing so.

31. What is a **mutual exclusion?**

It is a concept by means of which the single process temporarily excludes all others from using the shared resources.

32. Define the term **semaphore.**

A semaphore S is an integer variable that, apart from the initialization, can be accessed only through two standard atomic operations: P and V. The classical definitions of P and V are:

Wait (S): while S≤0 do skip;

S: = S–1;

Signal (S): S: = S+1.

A semaphore mechanism basically consists of two primitive operations SIGNAL and WAIT which operate on a special type of semaphore variable.

33. What is a **binary semaphore**?

A semaphore whose variable is allowed to take on only the values of 0(busy) and 1(free) is called a binary semaphore.

34. What is **Producers/Consumers problem**?

In general, Producers/Consumers may be stated as follows:
Given a set of cooperating processes, some of which "produce" data items (Producers) to be "consumed" by others (Consumers), with possible disparity between production and consumption rates.

35. Why is **interprocess synchronization** essential?

It is necessary to prevent timing errors due to concurrent accessing of shared resources, such as data structures or I/O devices by contending processes.

36. What is a **monitor**?

It provides the synchronization mechanism for sharing abstract data types.

37. List the disadvantages of semaphores.

(*a*) Semaphores are unstructured.

(*b*) They do not support data abstraction.

(*c*) They encourage interprocess communication via global variables that are protected only from changes of concurrency.

38. What are the advantages of using **critical regions**?

It enforces restricted usage of shared variables and prevents potential errors resulting from improper use of ordinary semaphores.

39. What is the disadvantage of using monitors?

It forces the users to live with whatever methods system designers may deem appropriate to access a given resource. These are unacceptable to system programmers.

40. What is a **Deadlock**?

A Deadlock is a situation where a group of processes are permanently blocked as a result of each process having acquired a subset of the resources needed for its completion and waiting for release of the remaining resources held by others in the same group thus making it impossible for any of the processes to proceed.

41. List the **necessary conditions for a deadlock** to take place.

A deadlock situation can rise if and only if the following four conditions hold simultaneously in a system: (*a*) Mutual exclusion (*b*) Hold and Wait (*c*) No preemption (*d*) Circular wait.

42. What is **contiguous memory allocation**?

Contiguous memory allocation means that each logical object is placed in a set of memory locations with strictly consecutive addresses.

43. What is **internal fragmentation**?

Wasting of memory within a partition, due to a difference in size of a partition and of the object resident within it, is called **internal fragmentation.**

44. What is **external fragmentation**?

Wasting of memory between partitions due to scattering of the free space into a number of discontinuous areas is called **external fragmentation.**

45. What is **PDT**?

Once partitions are defined, an operating system needs to keep track of their status, such as free or in use, for allocation purposes. Current partition status and attributes are often collected in a data structure called the **Partition Description Table (PDT).**

46. What are the two ways of allocating partitions in PDT?

(*a*) First-fit (*b*) Best-fit.

47. What is **Buddy system**?

An allocation-deallocation strategy, called the buddy system, facilitates merging of free space by allocating free areas with an affinity to recombine. Sizes of free blocks in a buddy system are usually an integer power of base 2.

48. What is **Segmentation**?

Segmentation is basically a multiple base-limit version of partitioned memory. As such, segmentation allows the breakup of the virtual address space of a process into several pieces, each of which can be assigned a different partition of the physical memory.

49. What are the merits and demerits of Segmentation?

The advantages are: (*a*) Elimination of internal fragmentation (*b*) Support for dynamic growth of segments (*c*) Protection (*d*) Sharing. The disadvantages are: (*i*) Management of segmented memory require comparatively more complex mechanisms than for either static or dynamic partitioning of memory and thus incurs higher operating system overhead. (*ii*) Several different segment base addresses may have to be used for address translations.

50. What is **Non-Contiguous memory allocation**?

Non-contiguous allocation means that memory is allocated in such a way that parts of a single logical object may be placed in non-contiguous areas of physical memory.

51. What is **virtual memory**?

The memory management scheme called virtual memory allows execution of processes when only portions of their address spaces are resident in the primary memory.

52. What is **demand paging/demand segmentation**?

Depending on whether paging or segmentation is used to manage physical memory, virtual memory management is referred to as demand paging or demand segmentation.

53. What is **paging**?

Paging is a memory management scheme that removes the requirement of contiguous allocation of the physical memory. Basically, the physical memory is divided into a number of fixed-size slots called page frames. The virtual address space of a process is also split into fixed-size blocks of the same size called **pages**.

54. What is **thrashing**?

A very high paging activity is called **thrashing**. A process is thrashing if it is spending more time paging than executing. Thrashing can cause severe performance problems.

55. What is the concept behind **overlays**?

A technique called **overlays** is sometimes used to allow a program to be larger than the amount of memory allocated to it. The idea of overlays is to keep in memory only those instructions and data that are needed at any given time.

56. What are **seek time, rotational latency and transfer time**?

Seek time is the time necessary for the read/write heads to travel to the target cylinder. **Rotational latency** is the time spent waiting for the target sector to appear under the read/write heads. **Transfer time** is the time necessary to transfer a sector between the disk and the memory buffer.

57. What is **disk fragmentation**?

Disk utilization refers to the percentage of disk space allocatable to users. One of the primary contributions to low disk utilization is disk fragmentation which occurs when free blocks are available but the system is unable to allocate them to requesting users.

58. What is meant by **file organization**?

File organization refers to the manner in which the records of a file are arranged on secondary storage. They are: (1) Sequential (2) Indexed Sequential (3) Direct and (4) Partitioned.

59. What are the characteristics of a **file**?

Files may be characterized by (1) Volatility (2) Activity and (3) Size.

60. What is a **thread**?

A thread, sometimes called a **lightweight process (LWP)**, is a basic unit of CPU utilization; it comprises of a thread ID, a program counter, a register set and a stack.

61. What is **multithreading**?

A multithreaded process contains several different flows of control within the same address space. The benefits of multithreading include increased responsiveness to the user, resource sharing within the process, economy and the ability to take advantage of multiprocessor architectures.

62. What are the **basic services** provided by an operating system?

(*a*) Program execution (*b*) I/O operations (*c*) File system manipulation (*d*) Communications (*e*) Error detection

63. What are **system calls?**

It provides the interface between a process and the operating system. These calls are generally available as assembly-language instructions, and they are usually listed in the various manuals used by the assembly-language programmers.

64. List the types of **system calls.**

(*a*) Process control (*b*) File management (*c*) Device management (*d*) Information maintenance (*e*) Communications.

65. What are the features of the **UNIX operating system?**

Portability, Machine-independence, Multi-user operations, Hierarchical file system, UNIX shell, Pipes and Filters, Utilities and Background processing.

66. What type of an operating system is the UNIX?

The UNIX operating system is a multi-programming, time-sharing, and multi-tasking system.

67. What are the components of **UNIX?**

Kernel, UNIX utilities and application software are the components of the UNIX.

68. List the **types of files in UNIX.**

Ordinary files, Directory files and Special files.

69. List the **various types of users in UNIX.**

System administrator, File owner, Group owner and other users.

70. What is a **Shell?**

A **Shell** is an intermediary program which interprets the commands that are typed at the terminal, and translates them into commands that the kernel understands.

71. List the various types of shells.

The shell runs like any other program under the UNIX system. Some of the popular shells are: Bourne shell, C shell, Korn shell and restricted shell.

72. Name the **directory** in which user will be working in UNIX.

/usr/bin

73. List the simple **directory commands** in UNIX.

(*a*) pwd (print working directory) command is used to display the full path-name of the current directory. $pwd<enter>

(*b*) The cd (Change directory) command changes the current directory to the directory specified.

(*c*) The mkdir (make directory) command is used to create directories.

(*d*) The rmdir (remove directory) removes the directory specified.

74. How will you list the contents of a directory in UNIX?

The ls command is used to display the names of files and subdirectories in a directory. $ls /user/games <enter>

75. What will be the output of ls –l command?

$ ls –l/user/games<enter>
total 3
- r w – r - - r - - 1 games staff 12 Apr 1 10:10 abc
- r w x r w x r w x 1 games staff 15 Apr 1 10:11 xyz
d r w x r w x r - - 2 games staff 30 Feb 1 11:10 pqr

There are nine columns above and they represent:

Column 1	*Column 2*	*Column 3*	*Column 4*	*Column 5*	*Column 6,7,8*	*Column 9*
File type	Number of Links	File owner	Group owner	File size (in bytes)	Day and time of last modification to the file.	Name file

The first character in column 1 can be '-' (ordinary file), 'd'(directory file) or special file.

76. How will you display the contents of a file?

The cat (concatenate) command displays the contents of the file specified.

$ cat data10 <enter>
example file

77. What is the use of **who** command?

The **who** command is used to display the names of all users who are currently logged in. The 'who am I' command displays the name of current users.

78. List the **Wildcard characters** in UNIX.

Character	*Purpose*
[ ]	Matches exactly one of a specified set of characters.
?	Matches exactly one character.
*	Matches none or one character or a string of more than one characters.

79. What is **FAP**?

File Access Permissions (FAP) refers to the permissions associated with a file with respect to the following:

(*a*) File owner (*b*) Group owner (*c*) Other users. The file read permission is denoted by 'r', write 'w' and execute 'x' in the first column of output of ls-l command.

80. What is the use of **chmod** command?

Access permissions associated with a file or directory can be changed using the **chmod** command. Permissions associated with a file can be changed only by the owner of the file.

81. What is **vi** editor?

The **vi** stands for visual editor, used to enter and edit text files containing data, documents or programs. It displays the contents of files on the screen, and allows the user to add, insert, delete or change parts of text.

82. How will you invoke the **vi** editor?

$ vi file name <enter>

83. What is a **filter**?

A filter is a program that takes its input from the standard input file, processes (or filters) it and sends its output to the standard output file. Examples of filters in the UNIX are: grep, cat, pg, wc, tr and cut.

84. What are the options available with **grep** filter?

The **grep** command has options which alter the output of the command. These are:

-n	This prints each line matching the pattern along with its line number.
-c	This prints only a count of the lines that match a pattern
-v	This prints out all those lines that do not match the pattern specified by regular expression

86. What is a **cut filter**?

It is useful when specific columns from the output of certain commands need to be extracted.

Example:

$ who > temp1<enter>

$ tr –s " " temp1 > temp2 <enter>

$ cut –d " " –f1 temp2 <enter>

87. What are the **options of cut filter**?

Cut –d	Specifies the column delimiter
Cut –c	Displays the character
Cut –f	Displays the columns specified

88. What is a **Pipe**?

Pipe is a feature by which the standard output of a command or user program can be sent as the standard input to another command or user program.

89. What is the use of the **echo** command?

The **echo** command is used to display messages on the screen.

90. How are **variables** handled in UNIX?

Variables in shell scripts do not have associated data types. That is, they are not declared to be integers or characters. All variables in UNIX are treated as character strings.

91. How are **comments** used in UNIX?

Comments which are required to be ignored by the shell can be included by prefixing them with the # symbol.

92. What are **environmental variables** in UNIX?

Theses are special variables created by the shell. Examples are PATH, HOME and LOGNAME

93. Give examples of a **multi-user operating system**.

UNIX, Solaris for SUN workstations, OS/2 for PS/2 machines and VMS (Virtual Memory System) for VAX machines.

94. What are the rules for handling **passwords** in UNIX?

A user password in UNIX cannot be less than 6 or more than 14 characters, but it can contain any character in the keyboard character set.

95. What are the **languages supported by UNIX**?

UNIX system supports a wide variety of languages namely C, PASCAL, ADA, COBOL, BASIC, LISP and PROLOG.

9 Computer Networks

1. Define the term **Computer Network.**

   We use the term **Computer Network** to mean an interconnected collection of autonomous computers.

2. What is the difference between **distributed system and computer network?**

   They key distinction between distributed system and computer network is that in a distributed system, the existence of multiple autonomous computers is transparent (i.e) not visible to the user. The user is not aware that there are multiple processors; it looks like a virtual uniprocessor. With a network, a user must explicitly log onto one machine, explicitly submit jobs remotely, explicitly move files around and generally handle all the network management personally.

3. What are the goals of a **network**?

   Resource sharing, high reliability and cost reduction.

4. What is **internetworking**?

   The connection of two or more networks is called **internetworking**.

5. What are the two types of design for the **communication subnet**?

   (*a*) Point-to-point channels (*b*) Broadcast channels.

6. What are the **Broadcast network** and **Point-to-point networks**?

   Broadcast networks have a single communication channel that is shared by all the machines on the network. Short messages, called packets in certain contexts, sent by any machine are received by all the others. A point-to-point network consists of many connections between individual pairs of machines. To go from the source to the destination, a packet on this type of network may have to first visit one or more intermediate machines.

7. What is **multicasting**?

   Some broadcast systems also support transmission to a subnet of the machines, something known as multicasting.

8. How are **networks** classified?

   Networks can be divided into LAN (Local Area Network), MAN (Metropolitan Area Network) and WAN (Wide Area Network)

9. What are the two **topologies** used for LAN?

   (*i*) Bus (*ii*) Ring.

10. What is an **Ethernet**?

    It is a bus based broadcast network with decentralized control operating at 10 or 100 Mbps.

11. What is a **host**?

A WAN consists of a collection of machines intended for running user (i.e. application) programs. These machines are called **Machine hosts**. The hosts are connected by a **communication subnet** or just **subnet**.

12. What are the two components of a **subnet**?

(*i*) Transmission lines (*ii*) Switching elements.

13. What is **internet**?

A collection of interconnected networks is called an **internetwork** or just **INTERNET**.

14. What is a **protocol**?

A protocol is an agreement between the communicating parties on how communication is to proceed. A set of layers and protocols is called a **Network Architecture**. A list of protocols used by a certain system, one protocol per layer, is called a **PROTOCOL STACK**.

15. What are connection-oriented and connectionless services?

Layers can offer two different types of services to the layers above them. They are:

(*a*) Connection-oriented service (*b*) Connectionless service

Connection-oriented service is modeled after the telephone system. To use a connection-oriented network service, the service user first establishes a connection, uses the connection and then releases the connection. Connectionless service is modeled after the postal system. Each service can be characterized by a quality of service.

16. Name the two **network architectures** considered important.

(*a*) OSI Reference Model (*b*) TCP/IP Reference Model.

17. What is the **OSI Model**?

This model is based on a proposal developed by the International Standards Organization (ISO) as a first step towards international standardization of the protocols used in the various layers. The model is called the Open Systems Interconnection Reference Model because it deals with connecting open systems (i.e.) the systems that are open for communication with other systems.

18. What is the **TCP/IP model**?

The TCP/IP (Transmission Control Protocol/Internet Protocol) Reference Model is the architecture which has the ability to connect multiple networks together in a seamless way.

19. What are the layers available in the OSI model and the TCP/IP model?

The seven layers of the OSI model are (1) Physical layer (2) Data link layer (3)Transport layer (4) Session layer (5) Presentation layer (6) Application layer (7) Network layer

20. What is the purpose of the **physical layer**?

It is used to transport a raw bit stream from one machine to another. Various physical media can be used for transmission namely (*a*) Magnetic media (*b*) Twisted pair (*c*) Baseband coaxial cable (*d*) Broadband coaxial cable (*e*) Fiber optics

21. What are the major problems in transmission lines?

(*i*) Attenuation (*ii*) Delay distortion (*iii*) Noise.

22. What is a **MODEM?**

A device that accepts a serial stream of bits as input and produces a modulated carrier as output (or vice versa) is called a **MODEM (Modulator-Demodulator).**

23. What is a **NULL MODEM?**

A MODEM is called NULL MODEM which connects the transmit line of one machine to the receive line of the other. It also crosses some of the other lines in a similar way. A NULL MODEM looks like a short cable.

24. What are the various **multiplexing** schemes?

FDM – Frequency Division Multiplexing

TDM – Time Division Multiplexing

WDM – Wavelength Division Multiplexing

25. Name the two **switching techniques.**

Circuit switching and Packet switching

26. Compare **Circuit switching and Packet switching.**

When a computer places a telephone call, the switching equipment within the telephone system seeks out a physical copper path all the way from the telephone line to the receiver's telephone. This technique is called the 'circuit switching'. Packet switching networks place a tight upper limit on block size, allowing packets to be buffered in router main memory instead of on disk. This switching network is well suited to handle interactive traffic.

27. What is **Narrowband ISDN?**

It is a circuit-switched digital system that is an incremental improvement over the current system.

28. What is **broadband ISDN?**

It represents a paradigm shift, since it is based on cell switching ATM technology. Various kinds of ATM switches exist including knockout switch, and the Batcher-Banyan switch. A Broadband ISDN is a digital virtual circuit for moving fixed size packets from service to destination at 155 Mbps.

29. What is meant by a **communication satellite?**

A communication satellite can be thought of as a big microwave repeater in the sky. It contains several transponders, each of which listens to some portion of the spectrum, amplifies the incoming signal, and then rebroadcasts it at another frequency, to avoid interference with the incoming signal.

30. Name the various **framing methods.**

(*a*) Character count (*b*) Starting and ending character with character stuffing

(*c*) Starting and ending flags with bit stuffing (*d*) Physical layer coding violations.

31. Name the elementary **data link protocols.**

(*a*) An Unrestricted simplex protocol

(*b*) A simplex stop and wait protocol

(*c*) A simplex protocol for a noisy channel

32. What is **Piggybacking**?

The technique of temporarily delaying outgoing acknowledgements so that they can be hooked onto the next outgoing data frame is known as **Piggybacking**.

33. What is the key issue in **broadcast network**?

In any broadcast network, the key issue is how to determine who gets to use the channel when there is competition for it. Broadcast channels are sometimes referred to as **multi-access channels** or **random access channels.**

34. What is **MAC**?

The protocol used to determine who goes next on a multi-access channel belongs to a sublayer of the data link layer called the MAC (Medium Access Control) sublayer. The MAC sublayer is important in LAN, which uses broadcast networks.

35. Compare **pure ALOHA** and **slotted ALOHA**.

In pure ALOHA, frames are transmitted completely at arbitrary time. Slotted ALOHA requires global time synchronization. The best we hope for channel utilization in pure ALOHA is 18 percent. For slotted ALOHA, it is 37 percent.

36. What is a **carrier sense protocol**?

Protocols in which stations listen for a carrier (i.e. transmission) and act accordingly are called **carrier sense protocols.**

37. What are the three classes of traffic supported by a protocol?

(*i*) Constant data rate connection-oriented traffic

(*ii*) Variable data rate connection-oriented traffic

(*iii*) Datagram traffic

38. What are **wireless LAN protocols**?

A system of portable computers that communicate by radio can be regarded as a "wireless LAN". These LANs requires special MAC (Medium Access Control) sublayer protocols.

39. Name the **IEEE** standard 802 for LAN and MAN.

IEEE standard 802.3 = Ethernet

IEEE standard 802.4 = Token Bus

IEEE standard 802.5 = Token Ring

IEEE standard 802.6 = Distributed Queue Dual Bus

IEEE standard 802.2 = Logical Link Control

40. What is a **Repeater**?

To allow larger networks, multiple cables can be connected by **repeaters**. A repeater is a physical layer device. It receives, amplifies and retransmits signals in both directions.

41. What is **Manchester Encoding**?

The receiver should determine the start, end or middle of each bit without reference to an external clock. Two such approaches are called **Manchester Encoding** and **Differential Manchester Encoding.**

42. What are the **functions** of various layers in the **OSI** reference model?

(*i*) The physical layer is concerned with transmitting raw bits over a communication channel. (*ii*) The main task of the data link layer is to take a raw transmission facility and transform it into a line that appears free of transmission error to the network layer. (*iii*) The network layer is concerned with controlling the operation of the subnet. (*iv*) The basic function of the transparent layer is to accept data from the session layer, split it up into smaller units if need be, pass these to the network layer, and ensure that the pieces all arrive correctly at the other end. (*v*) The session layer allows users on different machines to establish sessions between them. It provides two services namely token management and synchronization. (*vi*) The presentation layer is concerned with the syntax and semantics of the information transmitted. (*vii*) The application layer contains a variety of protocols that are commonly needed.

43. What are the properties required for a **routing algorithm**?

Correctness, simplicity, robustness, stability, fairness and optimality.

44. How are **routing algorithms** classified?

Routing algorithms are classified into two major classes namely non-adaptive and adaptive. Non-adaptive algorithms do not base their routing decisions on measurements or estimates of the current traffic and topology, whereas adaptive ones do. Adaptive algorithms can be further subdivided into centralized, isolated and distributed.

45. What is **flooding**?

It is an extreme form of isolated routing, in which every incoming packet is sent out on every outgoing line except the one it arrived on.

46. What is a **Client-server model**?

Communication always takes the form of request-reply pairs, always initiated by the clients, never by the server. This model is called the client-server model. In the client-server model, the client sends a request and the server sends a reply.

47. What is **RPC**?

Remote Procedure Call (RPC) can be viewed as a kind of connectionless session. In this model, when a client calls a remote procedure, the call is actually made to a local stub. This stub marshals the parameters and transmits a request message to the server. When the message arrives, the parameters are unmarshalled and the server procedure is called. The result traces the same path in the reverse direction.

48. What are **Plaintext** and **Cipher text**?

The messages to be encrypted known as the plaintext are transformed by a function that is parameterized by a key. The output of the encryption process, known as the Cipher text or Cryptogram, is then transmitted, often by messenger.

49. What is **Cryptanalysis**?

The art of breaking of ciphers is called **Cryptanalysis**. The art of devising ciphers (Cryptography) and breaking them (Cryptanalysis) is collectively known as **CRYPTOLOGY**.

50. What are the three ways of **data exchange**?

Simplex, Half-duplex and Full-duplex.

51. Name the various **topologies** for networks.

Bus topology, Star topology, Ring topology and Mesh network.

52. Compare **gateway** and **router**.

Gateways operate in all seven layers of the OSI model. Routers operate in the physical, data link and network layers.

53. What is a **brouter**?

They are hybrid devices that have the capability to combine the features of both bridges and routers.

54. What is a **Subnet**?

It is a generic term for a section of large networks which are usually separated by a bridge or router.

55. Define **bandwidth**.

Bandwidth is the amount of information that can be sent over a given transmission channel.

56. **Expand the following:** ICMP, ARP, RARP, TFTP, FTP, OSPF, SLIP and RIP.

ICMP – Internet Control Message Protocol

ARP – Address Resolution Protocol

RARP – Reverse Address Resolution Protocol

TFTP – Trivial File Transfer Protocol

FTP - File Transfer Protocol

OSPF – Open Shortest Path First Protocol

SLIP – Serial Line Internet Protocol

RIP – Routing Information Protocol

57. Why is the **HELLO protocol** preferred?

The HELLO protocol uses time instead of distance to determine optimal routing.

58. What is the special feature of **anonymous FTP**?

Anonymous FTP enables users to connect to a host without using a valid login and password.

59. Name the various types of servers.

File servers, database servers, transaction servers, web servers and object servers.

60. What is **multicast routing**?

Sending a message to a group is called multicasting and its routing algorithm is called **multicast routing**.

10 Digital Principles and Microprocessor

1. What is the main difference between **analog** and **digital operations**?

   The difference between analog and digital operations is the way the load line is used. With analog circuits, adjacent points on the load line may be used, so that the output voltage is continuous. Digital circuits are different. Almost all digital circuits are designed for two–state operation.

2. What is a **gate**?

   A digital circuit with one or more input voltages but only one output voltage.

3. Define **AND Gate** and **OR Gate**.

   A gate with two or more inputs is called AND gate. The output is high only when all inputs are high. A gate with two or more inputs is called OR gate where the output is high when any input is high.

4. What is an **inverter**?

   A gate with only one input and a complemented output.

5. Define a **Nibble**.

   A Nibble is a binary number with 4 bits.

6. What is **timing diagram**?

   The picture that shows the input–output waveforms of a logic circuit is called a **timing diagram**.

7. Define a **Truth Table**.

   A table that shows all of the input–output possibilities of a logic circuit.

8. What are the two fundamental approaches in logic design?

   Sum–of–products method and product–of–sums method.

9. State the **Double–Inversion rule**.

   It states that $\overline{\overline{A}} = A$, which shows that the double complement of a variable equals the variable.

10. How will you execute **dual property**?

    The dual property is obtained by changing the OR sign to an AND sign, and by complementing the 0 to get a 1.

11. What is a **Karnaugh map**?

    A Karnaugh map is a visual display of the fundamental products needed for a Sum–of–products solution.

12. What is a **Quad**?

A quad is a group of four one's that is horizontally or vertically adjacent.

13. State the **Don't care condition**.

An input–output condition that never occurs during normal operation is called **Don't care condition**.

14. What is a **Multiplexer**?

Multiplex means many into one. A multiplexer is a circuit with many inputs but only one output.

15. What is **Demultiplexer**?

Demultiplexer means one into many. A demultiplexer is a logic circuit with one input and many outputs.

16. What are **Decoder** and **Encoder**?

A Decoder is similar to a demultiplexer, with one exception–there is no data input. An Encoder converts an active input signal into a coded output signal.

17. What is **PAL**?

Programmable Array Logic (PAL) is a programmable array of logic gates on a single chip. It is different from a PROM because it has a programmable AND array and a fixed OR array.

18. What is a **Strobe**?

An input that disables or enables a circuit.

19. What is **Full–Adder** and **Half–Adder**?

Full–Adder is a logic circuit with three inputs and two outputs. The circuit adds 3 bits at a time, giving a sum and a carry output. Half–Adder is a logic circuit with two inputs and two outputs. It adds 2 bits at a time, producing a sum and a carry output.

20. Name the **Bipolar families**.

The following families belong to the bipolar category: (1) DTL (Diode–transistor logic) (2) TTL (Transistor–transistor logic) (3) ECL (Emitter–coupled logic).

21. Name the **MOS families**.

These families are in the metal-oxide semiconductor (MOS) category:

(*a*) PMOS = p-channel MOSFET

(*b*) NMOS = n-Channel MOSFET

(*c*) CMOS = Complimentary MOSFET

MOSFET stands for MOS field effect transistors.

22. What is a **bus**?

A bus is a group of wires that transmit binary data.

23. What is **noise immunity**?

The amount of noise voltages that causes unreliable operation.

24. What is **saturation delay time**?

The time delay encountered when a transistor tries to come out of the saturation region.

25. What is **CMOS**?

Complementary metal-oxide semiconductor (CMOS) devices are chips that combine p-channel and n-channel MOSFETs' in a push–pull arrangement.

26. What is a **flip-flop**?

An electronic circuit that has two stable states is called a flip-flop.

27. Define **Hold time**.

The minimum amount of time that data must be present after the clock trigger arrives is called **Hold time**.

28. Define **Edge Triggering**.

Edge Triggering is a circuit that responds only when the clock is in transition between its two voltage states.

29. What is a **clock**?

A clock is a periodic waveform that is used as a synchronizing signal in a digital system.

30. What is **Monostable**?

A Monostable is a circuit that has two output states, only one of which is stable.

31. What is a **shift register**?

A group of flip–flops connected in such a way that a binary number can be shifted into or out of the flip–flops is called a **shift register**.

32. Define a **ring counter**.

A ring counter is a basic–shift register with direct feedback—such that the contents of the register simply circulate around the register when the clock is running.

33. What is a **counter**?

A counter is probably one of the most useful and versatile subsystems in a digital system. A counter driven by a clock can be used to count the number of clock cycles.

34. What is **Dynamic memory**?

Dynamic memory is a memory whose contents must be restored periodically.

35. What are **Field-programmable** and **Mask-programmable**?

A PROM that can be programmed by the user is called field–programmable and a PROM that can be programmed only by the manufacturer is called mask–programmable.

36. What are **Hard saturation** and **Soft saturation**?

Hard saturation means the transistor has sufficient base current to be saturated under all operating conditions. Soft saturation means the transistor is barely saturated. The base current is just enough to operate the transistor at the upper end of the load line.

37. What is a **Microprocessor**?

A Microprocessor is a programmable logic device, designed with registers, flips–flops and timing elements. The microprocessor has a set of instructions designed internally to manipulate data and communicate with peripherals.

38. What is **Master–Slave triggering**?

A type of triggering using two cascade latches called the Master and the Slave. The master is clocked during the positive half cycle of the clock and the slave is triggered during the negative half cycle.

39. What is **stack pointer**?

The stack pointer is 16 bits long. All stack operations with the 8085 microprocessor use 16 bit register pairs. The stack pointer contains the address of the last data byte written into the stack.

40. What is **program counter**?

The program counter is 16 bits long to address up to 64 k of memory. It usually addresses the next instruction to be executed.

41. What are the **addressing modes** of 8085 microprocessor?

The 8085 microprocessor has the following five addressing modes:

(1) DIRECT (2) REGISTER (3) REGISTER INDIRECT

(4) IMPLIED OR INHERENT (5) IMMEDIATE.

42. Name the four one–byte 8085 **interrupt instructions.**

(1) DI (2) EI (3) RIM (4) SIM.

43. What are **SID** and **SOD**?

The Serial Input Data (SID) and Serial Output Data (SOD) lines are associated with the 8085 serial I/O transfer. The SOD line can be used to output the most significant bit of the accumulator. The SID signal can be input into the most significant bit of the accumulator.

44. What are **HOLD** and **HLDA** signals?

The HOLD and HLDA signals are used for the DMA (Direct Memory Access) type of data transfer. The HOLD function is acknowledged by the 8085 by placing a HIGH output on the HLDA pin.

45. What is **TRAP**?

TRAP is a nonmaskable interrupt, i.e., it cannot be enabled or disabled by an instruction. The TRAP has the highest property.

46. What are the advantages of **RIM instruction**?

RIM instruction can be used to read the interrupt pending bits in the accumulator. These bits can then be checked by software to determine whether any higher priority interrupts are pending.

47. What are the merits of **SIM instruction**?

SIM is a 1 byte instruction. This instruction reads the contents of the accumulator and enables or disables the interrupts according to the contents of the accumulator.

48. What is **DMA**?

The Direct Memory Access (DMA) is a process of communication or data transfer controlled by external peripherals. The situation, where the microprocessor controlled data transfer is too slow, the DMA is generally used.

49. Specify the general features of **INTEL 8086**.

The 8086 is Intel's first 16bit microprocessor. Its design is based on the 8080 but it is not directly compatible with 8080. The 8086 is designed using the HMOS technology and contains approximately 29000 transistors.

50. Name the six one bit flags of the 8086 microprocessor.

Auxiliary flag, carry flag, overflow flag, parity flag, zero flag and sign flag.

51. Name the three control bits flag of the 8086 microprocessor.

Direction flag, Interrupt flag and Trace flag.

52. Name the 8086 **Addressing modes.**

(*a*) Addressing modes for accessing **immediate** and **register** data.

(*b*) Addressing modes for accessing data in memory.

(*c*) Addressing modes for accessing I/O ports.

(*d*) Relative addressing mode.

(*e*) Implied Addressing mode.

53. What is **String Addressing Mode**?

The string mode uses index registers. It allows string memory operations.

54. What is **ASM–86**?

The ASM–86 is the assembler written by INTEL for the 8086 microprocessor.

55. Name the **ASM–86 assembler directives.**

(1) SEGMENT (2) ENDS (3) ASSUME (4) DUP

56. What is **Assembly Language Programming?**

It is a programming language in which the programmer can use mnemonic instruction codes, labels, and names to refer directly to their binary equivalents. An assembler is used to convert the assembly language into a machine language program.

11 DBMS, RDBMS and DDBMS

1. What is **DBMS**?

   A Database Management System **(DBMS)** consists of a collection of interrelated data and a set of programs to access those data. There are two other systems to manage database namely **RDBMS** (Relational Database Management System) and **DDBMS** (Distributed Database Management System).

2. What is a **database**?

   The Collection of data, usually referred to as the database, contains information about one particular enterprise.

3. What is the primary goal of a DBMS?

   The primary goal of a DBMS is to provide an environment that is both convenient and efficient to use in retrieving and storing database information.

4. What are the three levels of **data abstraction** in DBMS?

   Physical level, logical level, and view level.

5. What is the difference between the instance of the database and the database schema?

   The collection of information stored in the database at a particular moment is called an instance of the database. The overall design of the database is called the database schema.

6. What is **data independence**? How it is classified?

   The ability to modify a schema definition at one level without affecting a schema definition in the next higher level is called data independence. There are two levels of data independence:

   (1) Physical data independence
   (2) Logical data independence

7. What is a **Data model**?

   Underlying the structure of a database is the data model: a collection of conceptual tools for describing data, data relationships, data semantics and consistency constraints.

8. Name the various data models.

   Object-based logical model, Record-based logical model and Physical model.

9. What is an **E-R data model**?

   It is an object based logical model. It is based on a perception of a real world that consists of a collection of basic objects called entities and of relationships among these objects.

10. What is **mapping cardinality**?

    It expresses the number of entities to which another entity can be associated via a relationship set.

11. Name the three most widely accepted record-based data models.

Relational model, Network model and Hierarchical model.

12. How do we handle a database system?

A database system provides two different types of languages: one to specify the database schema and the other to express database queries and updates.

13. What is **DDL**?

A database schema is specified by a set of definitions expressed by a special language called **Data Definition Language (DDL)**.

14. What is a **data dictionary**?

The result of compilation of DDL statements is a set of tables that is stored in a special file called data dictionary or data directory. It contains metadata.

15. What is **DML**?

A data manipulation language (DML) is a language that enables users to access or manipulate data as organized by the appropriate data model.

16. Name the two **basic types of DML**.

Procedural DML and non-procedural DML

17. What is a **query**?

A query is a statement requesting retrieval of information. The portion of a DML that involves information retrieval is called a **query language**.

18. What is a **transaction**?

A transaction is a collection of operations that performs a single logical function in a database application. Each transaction is a unit of both atomicity and consistency.

19. What is a **storage manager**?

A storage manager is a program module that provides the interface between the low-level data stored in the database and the application programs and queries submitted to the system.

20. What is the role of a **DBA**?

The functions of the **DBA (Database Administrator)** include the schema definition, storage structure and access-method definition, schema and physical organization modification, access rights and integrity of data.

21. Name the four different types of **database system users.**

Application programmers, sophisticated users, specialized users and naïve users.

22. Name the **query processor components**.

DML compiler, Embedded DML pre-compiler, DDL interpreter and Query evaluation engine.

23. Name the **storage manager components**.

Authorization and integrity manager, Transaction manager, File manager and Buffer manager.

24. Name the three basic notions that the E-R data model employs.

The entity sets, relationship sets and attributes.

25. How are **attributes** classified?

Simple and Composite attributes, Single-valued and Multivalued attributes, Null attributes and Derived attributes.

26. What is a **Super key**?

A Super key is a set of one or more attributes that, taken collectively, allows us to identify uniquely an entity in the entity set.

27. Compare a **Weak entity set** and a **Strong entity set**.

An entity set may not have sufficient attributes to form a primary key. Such an entity set is termed as a weak entity set. An entity set that has a primary key is termed a strong entity set.

28. Distinguish between **Specialization** and **Generalization**.

Specialization and Generalization define a containment relationship between a higher-level entity set and one or more lower-level entity sets. Specialization is the result of taking a subset of a higher-level entity set to form a lower-level entity set. Generalization is the result of taking the union of two or more disjoint (lower-level) entity sets to produce a higher-level entity set.

29. What is the drawback of the **E-R model**?

One limitation of the E-R model is that it cannot express relationships among relationships. The solution is to use aggregation.

30. What forms the basis for deriving a relational-database design from an E-R diagram?

Converting of database representation from an E-R diagram to a table format is the basis for deriving a relational-database design from an E-R diagram.

31. Specify the distinctions among the terms **primary key, candidate key** and **super key**.

A **super key** is a set of one or more attributes that, taken collectively, allows us to identify uniquely an entity in the entity set. Super keys for which no proper subset is a super key is called **candidate keys**. A **primary key** is used to denote a **candidate key** that is chosen by the database designer as the principal means of identifying entities within an entity set.

32. What is **relational algebra**?

Relational algebra is a procedural query language. It consists of a set of operations that take one or two relations as input and produce a new relation as their results.

33. Name the fundamental operations in the **relational algebra**.

Select, Project, Union, Set difference, Cartesian product and Rename; there are other operations like set intersection, natural join, division and assignment.

34. What are **unary operations** and **binary operations**?

The select, project and rename operations are called unary operations, because they operate on one relation. The other three operations are pairs of relations and are, therefore, called binary operations.

35. Define a **view**.

Any relation that is not part of the logical model but is made visible to a user as a virtual relation is called a **view**.

36. What are the three clauses supported by **SQL**?

'Select', 'From' and 'Where'.

37. Name the various kinds of set operations.

The Union operation, The Intersect operation and The Except operation.

38. What is an **aggregate function**?

Aggregate functions are functions that take a collection of values as input and return a single value. SQL offers five built-in aggregate functions: Average, Minimum, Maximum, Total and Count.

39. Define a **host language** and **embedded SQL**.

A language in which SQL queries are embedded is referred to as a **host language** and the SQL structures permitted in the host language constitute the **embedded SQL**. An embedded SQL program must be processed by a special preprocessor prior to compilation.

40. What is **QBE**?

Query-by-Example (QBE) is the name of both a data-manipulation language and the database system that included this language.

41. Define the term **Integrity constraints**.

Integrity Constraints provide a means of ensuring that changes made to the database by authorized users do not result in a loss of data consistency. Thus Integrity Constraints guard against accidental damage to the database.

42. What is the use of **check** clause in SQL?

The **check** clause permits the schema designer to specify a predicate that must be satisfied by any value assigned to a variable whose type is the domain.

43. What is **Referential Integrity**?

Referential Integrity is a condition which ensures that a value that appears in one relation for a given set of attributes also appears for a certain set of attributes in another relation.

44. Define the term **Assertion**.

An Assertion is a predicate expressing a condition that we wish the database always to satisfy. Domain constraints and Referential-integrity constraints are special form of assertions.

45. Give the syntax of an **assertion**.

Create assertion <assertion-name> check <predicate>.

46. What is a **trigger**?

A trigger is a statement that is executed automatically by the system as a side effect of a modification to the database.

47. What are the requirements for trigger mechanism?

(*a*) Specifying the conditions under which the trigger is to be executed.

(*b*) Specifying the actions to be taken when the trigger executes.

48. What is **Functional Dependency (FD)?**

Functional Dependency (FD) is a particular kind of constraint. It is a generalization of the notion of key: Let A⊆R and B⊆R. The FD A→B holds on R if, in any legal relation r(R), for all pairs of tuples t1 and t2 in r such that t1 [A] =t2 [A], it is also the case that t1 [B] =t2 [B]. Functional dependencies allow us to express constraints that we cannot express using super keys.

49. When is FD said to be **trivial**?

Some FD is said to be trivial because they are satisfied by all relations.

50. State the rules of inference for **FD**.

(*a*) Reflexivity rule (*b*) Augmentation rule (*c*) Transitivity rule.

51. What are the pitfalls in **Relational-database design**?

(*a*) Repetition of information.

(*b*) Inability to represent certain information.

52. When is a relation called **legal**?

We say a relation is **legal** if it satisfies all rules or constraints that we impose on our database.

53. What is **Lossless-join decomposition**?

Let C represent a set of constraints on the database. A decomposition {R1, R2,....Rn} of a relation schema R is a lossless-join decomposition for R if, for all relations r on schema R that are legal under C, r = πR1(r)XπR2(r)X····πRn(r)

54. What is **Normalization**?

Normalization is a process of analyzing the given relation schemas. Normalization applies functional dependencies and primary key to reduce redundancy, insertion, deletion and updation anomalies.

55. What is **1NF (Normal Form)**?

The domain of attribute must include only atomic values (i.e) simple, indivisible values.

56. What is **2NF**?

A relation schema R is in 2NF if and only if it is in 1NF and every non-prime attribute A in the relation schema R is fully functionally dependent on the primary key.

57. What is **BCNF (Boyce-Codd Normal Form)**?

A relation schema R is in BCNF if and only if it is in 3NF and satisfies additional constraints that for every functional dependency X→A, X must be a candidate key.

58. How is **checkpoint** useful in DBMS?

By taking checkpoints, the DBMS can reduce the amount of work to be done during restart in the event of subsequent crashes.

59. What is **object-oriented data model?**

It is an adaptation to database systems of the object-oriented programming paradigm. It is based on the concept of encapsulating in an object the data, and the code that operates on those data.

60. Name the languages used to implement object orientation.

Data manipulation language, Persistent programming language.

61. Define **object-relational systems.**

Systems that provide object-oriented extensions to relational systems are called **Object-relational systems.**

62. Define **Persistent programming languages.**

An existing object-oriented programming language can be extended to deal with databases. Such languages are called **Persistent programming languages.**

63. What is **Nesting** and **Unnesting**?

The transformation of a nested relation into the first normal form is called Unnesting. The reverse process of transforming a first normal form into a nested relation is called nesting. Nesting can be carried out by an extension of grouping in SQL.

64. Define an **Index of a file.**

An Index of a file in the system works in much the same way as a catalog for a book in a library. There are two basic kinds of indices: (1) Order Indices (2) Hash Indices.

65. What is **Query processing**?

Query processing refers to the range of activities involved in extracting data from a database.

66. What are the steps involved in processing a query?

Parsing and translation, optimization and evaluation.

67. What is a **transaction**? What are its properties?

A transaction is a unit of program execution that accesses and possibly updates various data items. The database system maintains the following properties of transactions: (*a*) Atomicity (*b*) Consistency (*c*) Isolation (*d*) Durability.

68. List the various **states** which a **transaction** can occupy.

Active, partially committed, failed, aborted and committed are the various states. Out of these a transaction must occupy one of the states.

69. What is a **spatial database**?

Spatial databases include geographic databases, which store maps and associated information, and computer-aided design databases, which store information such as integrated-circuit or building designs.

70. What is **Data Mining**?

The term **Data Mining** refers loosely to finding relevant information, or **discovering knowledge**, from a large volume of data. Data mining attempts to discover statistical rules and patterns automatically from data.

71. What are the two important classes of problem in data mining?

Classification and Association rules.

72. What is meant by a **Data Warehouse**?

A **Data Warehouse** is a repository (or archive) of information gathered from multiple sources, stored under a unified scheme, at a single site. The issues to be addressed in building a warehouse are: (*a*) When and how to gather data (*b*) What schema to use (*c*) How to propagate updates (*d*) What data to summarize.

73. Name the two types of **spatial databases**?

Design databases and Geographic databases.

74. Define a **distributed database**.

A **distributed database** is a collection of data which belong logically to the same system but are spread over the sites of a computer network.

75. List the advantages of distributed database.

The main advantages are: (*a*) Organizational and Economic reasons (*b*) Interconnection of existing databases (*c*) Incremental growth (*d*) Reduced communication overhead (*e*) Reliability and availability.

76. What is **DDBMS**?

A Distributed Database Management System **(DDBMS)** supports the creation and maintenance of distributed databases. An important property of DDBMS is whether they are homogeneous or heterogeneous.

77. What is **distribution transparency**?

Distribution transparency provides the independence of programs from the distribution of the database. Different levels of distribution transparency can be provided by a DDBMS; at each level, different aspects of the real distribution of data are hidden from the application programmers.

78. What are the four phases in the design of a distributed database?

(1) The design of the global schema

(2) The design of fragmentation

(3) The design of allocation

(4) The design of physical structures at each site

79. What is **Database administration**?

It refers to a variety of activities for the development, control, maintenance and testing the software of the database application.

80. What is a **catalog**?

Catalogs are small, distributed databases, whose distribution and allocation are not constrained. Catalogs of distributed databases store all the information which is useful to the system for accessing data correctly and efficiently and for verifying that users have the appropriate access rights to them.

81. Name the three classes of **concurrency control algorithms**.

(*a*) Two-phase locking (*b*) Timestamps (*c*) Optimistic methods.

82. What are the rules to be observed for the successful concurrent execution of transaction?

(*a*) Transactions are well-formed.

(*b*) Compatibility rules for locking are observed.

(*c*) Each transaction does not request new locks after it has released a lock.

83. What are the approaches to store a relation r in a distributed database?

(1) Replication (2) Fragmentation (3) Replication and Fragmentation are the three approaches for storing the relation 'r' in the distributed database.

84. What is the usage of **commit protocol**?

To ensure atomicity, a transaction T must either commit at all sites, or it must abort at all sites. To ensure this property, the transaction coordinator of T must execute a commit protocol. The two types of commit protocols in practice are: (1) Two-phase commit protocol (2PC) and (2) Three-phase commit protocol (3PC).

85. What are the two types of transactions supported by a **multidatabase system**?

(1) Local transactions (2) Global transactions.

86. Name the **unary operations** in relational algebra.

PROJECTION and SELECTION.

87. Compare **PRODUCT** and **JOIN** operations.

PRODUCT and JOIN operations are not the same. Concatenation of every row in one relation with every row in another is PRODUCT operation. Concatenation of rows from one relation and related rows from another is JOIN operation.

88. List the tools of **ORACLE**.

(*i*) SQL *PLUS (*ii*) PL/SQL (*iii*) Forms (*iv*) Reports.

89. Name the **Oracle's database language**.

SQL (Structured Query Language).

90. What are the **commands** supported by **SQL**?

(*a*) Data Definition Language (DDL)--Create, Alter, Drop commands.

(*b*) Data Manipulation Language (DML)--Insert, Select, Update and Delete commands.

(*c*) Transaction Control Language (TCL)--Commit, Save point, Rollback commands.

(*d*) Data Control Language (DCL)--Grant and Revoke commands.

91. What is **SQL *PLUS**?

SQL *PLUS is an oracle specific program which accepts SQL commands and PL/SQL blocks and executes them. SQL *PLUS enables manipulation of SQL commands and PL/SQL blocks.

92. Name the **oracle internal data types.**

(*a*) Char data type (*b*) Varchar2 data type (*c*) Long data type (*d*) Number data type

(*e*) Date data type (*f*) Long raw data type (*g*) Raw data type

12 Test Yourself (Objective Type Questions)

CHOOSE THE BEST ANSWER

1.
```
#define MAX(x,y) ((x)>(y)?(x):(y))
main()
{
int x=5, y=5;
printf ("%d", MAX(++x,++y));
}
```
The output of the program is:

(*a*) 7 (*b*) 5 (*c*) 6 (*d*) none of these

2. Given the following definitions, what will be the value of r?
```
int *p, *q, r;
int values[30];
p=&values[0];
q=values+29;
r=++q-p;
```
(*a*) address of q minus p
(*b*) number of elements in the array
(*c*) (value pointed by q)+1-(value pointed by p)
(*d*) none of these

3. What will be the output of the program?
```
#include <stdio.h>
static int =5;
main()
{
int sum=0;
do
{
sum+=(1/i);
}while(0<i--);
printf ("%d", sum);
}
```
(*a*) sum of the series is printed
(*b*) compilation error
(*c*) runtime error
(*d*) none of these

4.
```
#include <stdio.h>
enum mode={green, red, orange, blue, white};
main()
{
green = green+1;
printf ("%d%d",green,red);
}
```

The output of the program will be:

(*a*) 1,1 (*b*) 0,1
(*c*) no output, error in compilation (*d*) none of these

5. What is the size of ptr1 and ptr2?

```
Struct x{
Int j;
Char k[100];
Unsigned I;
};
int *ptr1;
struct x *ptr2;
```

(*a*) same (*b*) 2, 104
(*c*) 2, undefined for memory is not allowed (*d*) 2, 4

6. What is the output of the following program?

```
#include <stdio.h>
main( )
{
int i=0;
switch(i)
{
case 0: i++;
case 1: i++2;
case 2: ++i;
}
printf (“%d”, i++);
}
```

The output of the program is:

(*a*) 1 (*b*) 3 (*c*) 4 (*d*) 5

7. If i=5, what is the output for printf (“%d%d%d”, ++i,i,i++)?

(*a*) 5,6,7 (*b*) 6,6,7 (*c*) 7,6,5 (*d*) 6,5,6

8. For the following code, how many times is the **printf** function executed?

```
int i,j;
for (i=0;i<=10;i++);
for (j=0;j<=10;j++);
printf(“i=%d,j=%d\n”,i,j);
```

(*a*) 121 (*b*) 11 (*c*) 10 (*d*) none of these

9. What is the output generated for the following code?

```
#define square (a) (a*a)
printf(“%d”,square(4+5));
```

(*a*) 81 (*b*) 4 (*c*) 29 (*d*) none of these

10. For the following statement, find the values generated for p and q.

```
int p=0, q=1;
p=q++;
p=++q;
p=q--;
p=--q;
```

(*a*) 1,1 (*b*) 0,0 (*c*) 3,2 (*d*) 1,2

11. What is the output generated by the following program?

```
#include <stdio.h>
main()
{
int a, count;
int func(int);
for(count=1;count<=5;++count)
{
a=func(count);
printf("%d",a);
}}
int func(int x)
{
int y;
y=x*x;
return (y);
}
```

(*a*) 1234567 (*b*) 2516941 (*c*) 9162514 (*d*) 1491625

12. C programming allows

(*a*) only call by value

(*b*) only call by reference

(*c*) both (*a*) and (*b*)

(*d*) only call by value and sometimes call by reference

13. The statement "The size of a struct is always equal to the sum of the sizes of its members" is

(*a*) valid (*b*) invalid

(*c*) can't say (*d*) depends on struct

14. How many X's are printed?

```
for (i=0;j=10;i<j;i++,j--)
printf("X");
```

(*a*) 10 (*b*) 5 (*c*) 4 (*d*) none of these

15. X=malloc(Y). Which of the following statement is correct?

(*a*) X is the size of the memory allocated

(*b*) Y points to the memory allocated

(*c*) X points to the memory allocated

(*d*) none of these

16. How many variables are required to swap two numbers using a temporary variable and without using a temporary variable?

(*a*) 3,2 (*b*) 3,3 (*c*) 2,3 (*d*) 2,2

17. Which of the following is valid?

(*a*) Pointers can be added

(*b*) Pointers can be subtracted

(*c*) Integers can be added to pointers

(*a*) all are correct (*b*) (*a*) is correct (*c*) (*a*) and (*b*) (*d*) (*a*) and (*c*)

18.
```
int *i;
float *f;
char *c;
```
Which are the valid castings?

(*a*) (int) &c (*b*) (float) &c (*c*) (char) &ib (*d*) none of these

19.
```
int i=20;
printf ("%x", i);
```
What is the output?

(*a*) x14 (*b*) 14 (*c*) 20 (*d*) none of these

20.
```
main()
{
char *name = "name";
change (name);
printf("%s",name);
}
change (char *name)
{
char *nm="newname";
name=nm;
}
```
What is the output?

(*a*) name (*b*) newname

(*c*) name=nm is not valid (*d*) function call invalid

21.
```
#define max(a,b) (a>b?b:a)
#define square(x) x*x;
int i=2, j=3, k=1;
printf("%d%d", max(i,j), square(k));
```
What is the output?

(*a*) 32 (*b*) 23 (*c*) 31 (*d*) 13

22. Which is the valid declaration?

(*a*) #typedef struct {int i;}in; (*b*) typedef struct in {int i;};

(*c*) #typedef struct int{int i;}; (*d*) typedef struct {int i;}in;

23. What is the optimum number of operations for 2*(X**3)+3*(X**2)+5*X+5?

(*a*) 3 multiplications, 3 additions
(*b*) 2 multiplications, 2 additions
(*c*) 3 multiplications, 4 additions
(*d*) 4 multiplications, 3 additions

24.
```
main()
{char a[2];
*a[0]=7;
*a[1]=5;
printf("%d",&a[1]-a);
}
```
The output is:

(*a*) 1
(*b*) illegal initialization
(*c*) 2
(*d*) none of these

25.
```
int *p;
i=10;
p=i;
printf("%d",*p);
```
The output is:

(*a*) error (*b*) 10 (*c*) i (*d*) none of these

26. Is main() in C programming

(*a*) a function (*b*) a procedure (*c*) a declaration (*d*) a header file

27. Is there any difference between for(i=0;i<10;i++) and for(i=10;i<n;++i) ?

(*a*) no
(*b*) yes
(*c*) depends on 'i'
(*d*) depends on the program

28. How many 'for' loops are required to carry out a matrix multiplication?

(*a*) 3 (*b*) 4 (*c*) 2 (*d*) 1

29. How will you represent *a[i]?

(*a*) *(a+i) (*b*) (*a+i) (*c*) (a+*i) (*d*) (*a+*i)

30.
```
int count=11;
while (– –count+1)
printf("count down is %d\n",count);
```
How many times is the printf statement executed?

(*a*) 11 (*b*) 10 (*c*) 8 (*d*) none of these

31. How many bytes of memory will the following arrays need?

Char s[80], char s[80][10], int d[10], float d[10][5]

(*a*) 80,800,20,200
(*b*) 80,80,20,200
(*c*) 80,800,10,50
(*d*) 80,800,10,15

32. Give the name of the standard library function for the following: string length, string compare, string copy and string concatenation.

(*a*) strlen, strcmp, strcpy, strcat
(*b*) stringlen, stringcmp, strcpy, strcat
(*c*) strlen,strcompare,stringcopy,strcat
(*d*) strlen[], strcmp[],strcpy[],strcat[]

33. Suppose i and j are both integer type variables, and j has been assigned a value of 5. Find the value of i for the following expressions:

(*a*) i=2*j-2*j/5 (*b*) i=j/2 (*c*) i=2*j/2 (*d*) i=(2*j)/2

(*a*) 8,2,4,2 (*b*) 8,0,4,5 (*c*) 8,2,0,0 (*d*) none of these.

34. Which of the following represents scope resolution operator?

(*a*) :: (*b*) * (*c*) & (*d*) none of these

35. Which of the following is called a class member access operator?

(*a*) & (*b*) dot operator (*c*) [ ] (*d*) **

36. A constructor that accepts no parameters is called

(*a*) default constructor
(*b*) parameterized constructor
(*c*) overloaded constructor
(*d*) implicit constructor

37. Which of the following operators cannot be overloaded?

(*a*) dot operator (*b*) + (*c*) – (*d*) *

38. Which of the following operators is not related to a friend function?

(*a*) = (*b*) + (*c*) – (*d*) *

39. A function declared in a base class that has no definition relative to the base class is called

(*a*) pure virtual function
(*b*) virtual function
(*c*) friend class
(*d*) friend function

40. Which of the following is used to represent an object that invokes a member function?

(*a*) 'this'
(*b*) scope resolution operator
(*c*) #symbol
(*d*) assignment operator

41. Which of the following access specifiers are accessible from own class, from derived class and from objects outside the class?

(*a*) public
(*b*) protected
(*c*) private
(*d*) private and public

42. The destructor for the class integer can be defined as:

(*a*) ~integer(){} (*b*) ~integer{}() (*c*) ~integer (*d*) integer()

43. The process of creating a specific class from a class template is called

(*a*) instantiation
(*b*) instant class
(*c*) function template
(*d*) template instantiation

44. The declarations for the manipulators are available in:

(*a*) iostream.h (*b*) stdio.h
(*c*) iomanip.h (*d*) conio.h

45. Which of the following involves context switch?

(*a*) SPOOL (*b*) processor (*c*) thread (*d*) none of these

46. For 1MB memory, the number of address lines required is:

(*a*) 11 (*b*) 16 (*c*) 22 (*d*) 24

47. Semaphore is used for

(*a*) synchronization (*b*) dead-lock (*c*) exception (*d*) (*b*) and (*c*)

48. Which holds true for the following statement?

Class C: Public A, Public B

(*a*) 2 member in class A, B should not have the same name
(*b*) 2 member in class A, C should not have the same name
(*c*) both a & b
(*d*) none of these

49. Piggybacking is a technique for

(*a*) flow control (*b*) error control (*c*) acknowledgement (*d*) (*a*) and (*b*)

50. In a signed magnitude notation, what is the minimum value that can be represented with 8 bits?

(*a*) –128 (*b*) –255 (*c*) –127 (*d*) 0

51. In the following statement, what is the value of may?
Enum = {jan=1,feb=4,april,may}

(*a*) 4 (*b*) 5 (*c*) 6 (*d*) none of these

52. What is the output for the following C program?

```
i=20,k=0;
for(j=1;j<i;j=1+4*(i/j))
{
k+=j<10?4:3;
}
printf(“%d”,k);
```

(*a*) k=4 (*b*) 4 (*c*) 3 (*d*) none of these

53. Find the output:

```
int i=10;
main()
{
int i=20,n;
for(n=0;n<=i;)
{
```

```
int i=10;
i++;
}
printf("%d",i);
```

(*a*) i=20; (*b*) 20 (*c*) 10 (*d*) none of these

54. What is the sizeof(long int)?

(*a*) 4 bytes (*b*) 2 bytes
(*c*) 8 bytes (*d*) depends on compiler

55. The main() in C must be

(*a*) The first function in the program (*b*) The first statement in the program
(*c*) Written anywhere in the program (*d*) None of these

56. Which of the following about automatic variables within a function is correct?

(*a*) its type must be declared before using the variable
(*b*) they are legal
(*c*) they are not initialized to zero
(*d*) they are global

57. Write one statement equivalent to the following two statements: x=sqr(*a*); return(x);

(*a*) return(sqr(*a*)); (*b*) printf("sqr(*a*)");
(*c*) return(a*a*a); (*d*) printf("%d",sqr(*a*));

58. Which of the following about the C comments is INCORRECT?

(*a*) comments can go over multiple lines.
(*b*) comments can start anywhere in the line.
(*c*) a line can contain comments without any language statements.
(*d*) comments can occur within comments.

59. What is the value of y in the following code?

```
x=7; y=0;
if(x=6) y=7;
else y=1;
```

(*a*) 7 (*b*) 0 (*c*) 1 (*d*) none of these

60. What value is returned by the following function?

```
Conver(int t)
{
int u;
u=5/9*(t-32);
return (u);
}
```

(*a*) 15 (*b*) 0 (*c*) 16.1 (*d*) 29

61. Which of the following is INCORRECT?

(*a*) automatic variables are automatically initialized to 0.

(*b*) static variables are automatically initialized to 0.
(*c*) the address of a register variable is not accessible.
(*d*) static variables cannot be initialized with any expression.

62. The operator used for exponentiation is

(*a*) ** (*b*) ^ (*c*) % (*d*) #

63. Which of the following is INVALID?

(*a*) a+=b (*b*) a*=b (*c*) a>>=b (*d*) a**=b

64. How many times does the following loop occur?

```
a=0;
while(a<5)
printf("%d",a++);
```

(*a*) infinite (*b*) 5 (*c*) 4 (*d*) 6

65. How many times does the following loop occur?

```
for(i=0;i=10;i+=2)
printf("hai");
```

(*a*) 10 (*b*) 2 (*c*) 5 (*d*) none of these

66. Which of the following is INCORRECT regarding a recursive function?

(*a*) calls itself (*b*) is equivalent to a loop
(*c*) has a termination condition (*d*) does not have a return value at all

67. Find the odd one out among the following.

(*a*) malloc() (*b*) calloc() (*c*) free() (*d*) realloc()

68. Consider the following program:

```
main()
{
int a[5]={1,3,6,7,0};
int *b;
b=&a[2];
}
```

The value of b[–1] is

(*a*) 1 (*b*) 3 (*c*) –6 (*d*) none of these

69. The format used for hexadecimal is

(*a*) %d (*b*) %o (*c*) %x (*d*) %u

70. What is the output?

```
main()
{int x=5,*p;
p=&x;
printf("%d",++*p);
}
```

(*a*) 5 (*b*) 6 (*c*) 0 (*d*) none of these

71. int *a[5] refers to

(*a*) array of pointers
(*b*) pointer to an array
(*c*) pointer to a pointer
(*d*) none of these

72. Which of the following is not a group function?

(*a*) avg() (*b*) sqrt() (*c*) sum() (*d*) max()

73. Once defined, how long will a variable remain so in SQL *PLUS?

(*a*) until the database is shutdown
(*b*) until the instance is shutdown
(*c*) until the statement ends
(*d*) until the session ends

74. Which function below can best be categorized as similar in function to an IF-THEN-ELSE statement?

(*a*) SQRT
(*b*) DECODE
(*c*) NEW-TIME
(*d*) ROWIDTOCHAR

75. Which of the following two orders are used by ORDER BY clause?

(*a*) ABS, ASC (*b*) ASC, DESC (*c*) ABS, DESC (*d*) none of these

76. Which of the following is not a feature of a cursor FOR loop?

(*a*) record type declaration
(*b*) opening and parsing of SQL statements
(*c*) fetches records from cursor
(*d*) requires exit condition to be defined

77. The command used to open a cursor FOR LOOP is

(*a*) open (*b*) fetch (*c*) parse (*d*) none of these

78. What happens when rows are found using a FETCH statement?

(*a*) It causes the cursor to close
(*b*) It causes the cursor to open
(*c*) It loads the current rows values into variables
(*d*) It creates the variables to hold the current row values

79. Which procedure can be used to create a customized error message?

(*a*) RAISE_ERROR
(*b*) SQLERRM
(*c*) RAISE_APPLICATION_ERROR
(*d*) RAISE_SERVER_ERROR

80. What is the CPU scheduling algorithm used by the UNIX operating system?

(*a*) preemptive
(*b*) non-preemptive
(*c*) preemptive with dynamic priority
(*d*) preemptive with static priority

81. The UNIX operating system is based on

(*a*) monolithic (*b*) micro-kernel (*c*) multithreading (*d*) multitasking

82. After serving a page fault, the control returns to

(*a*) the next instruction
(*b*) depends on operating system
(*c*) the same instruction but the program halts
(*d*) the same instruction but the program hangs

83. A program written using the data structure .... results in minimum page faults.

(*a*) stack (*b*) hash queue
(*c*) priority queue (*d*) priority lists

84. Virtual memory is implemented by

(*a*) simple paging
(*b*) demand paging
(*c*) static partitioned memory management
(*d*) dynamic partitioned memory management

85. WINDOWS NT is designed as

(*a*) RISC (*b*) CISC (*c*) both (*a*) and (*b*) (*d*) none of these

86. Web client talks to web server through

(*a*) TCP port 80 (*b*) TCP port 21 (*c*) UDP port 80 (*d*) UDP port 21.

87. DLL stands for

(*a*) dynamic link library (*b*) dynamic language library
(*c*) dynamic load library (*d*) none of these

88. POST-BLOCK trigger is a

(*a*) navigational trigger (*b*) key trigger
(*c*) transactional trigger (*d*) none of these

89. Which of the following packaged procedure is UNRESTRICTED?

(*a*) CALL_INPUT (*b*) CLEAR-BLOCK (*c*) EXECUTE_QUERY (*d*) USER-EXIT

90. Identify the RESTRICTED packaged procedure from the following:

(*a*) USER_EXIT (*b*) MESSAGE (*c*) BREAK (*d*) EXIT_FORM

91. What is SQL*FORMS?

(*a*) It is a 4GL tool for developing and executing oracle based interactive applications.
(*b*) SQL*FORMS is a 3GL tool for connecting to the database.
(*c*) SQL*FORMS is a reporting tool.
(*d*) none of these

92. What is a DATABLOCK?

(*a*) set of extents (*b*) set of segments
(*c*) smallest database storage unit (*d*) none of these

93. A Transaction ends

(*a*) only when it is committed (*b*) only when it is rolled back
(*c*) when it is committed or rolled back (*d*) none of these

94. PL/SQL supports datatypes(s)

(*a*) scalar datatype (*b*) composite datatype (*c*) both (*a*) and (*b*) (*d*) none of these

95. Find the odd datatype out of the following

(*a*) VARCHAR2 (*b*) RECORD (*c*) BOOLEAN (*d*) RAW

96. Find the ODD one out of the following

(*a*) OPEN (*b*) CLOSE (*c*) INSERT (*d*) FETCH

97. Which of the following is NOT CORRECT about cursor?

(*a*) cursor is a named private SQL area
(*b*) cursor holds temporary results
(*c*) cursor is used for retrieving multiple rows
(*d*) SQL uses implicit cursors to retrieve rows

98. Which of the following is NOT VALID in PL/SQL?

(*a*) Select...into (*b*) Update (*c*) Create (*d*) Delete

99. Is it possible to modify a datatype of a column when the column contains data in a table?

(*a*) yes (*b*) no
(*c*) depends on data (*d*) depends on datatype

100. The DML statements are

(*a*) INSERT (*b*) SELECT (*c*) UPDATE (*d*) all of these

101. What is the SYSTEM VARIABLE used to refer DATABASE time?

(*a*) $$dbtime$$ (*b*) $$time$$ (*c*) $$date$$ (*d*) none of these

102. The sequence of events that takes places while starting a database is

(*a*) database opened, file mounted, instance started
(*b*) instance started, database mounted, database opened
(*c*) database opened, instance started, file mounted
(*d*) none of these

103. The status of the rollback segment can be viewed through

(*a*) DBA_SEGMENTS (*b*) DBA_ROLES
(*c*) DBA_FREE_SPACES (*d*) DBA_ROLLBACK_SEG

104. What file is read by ODBC to load drivers?

(*a*) ODBC.INI (*b*) ODBC.DLL (*c*) ODBCDRV.INI (*d*) none of these

105. Which of the following is a feature of ERP software?

(*a*) ERP is packaged software (*b*) It is flexible
(*c*) It integrates information (*d*) It supports CRM

106. ERP stands for

(*a*) Enterprise resource planning (*b*) Entire resource planning
(*c*) Enterprise requirements planning (*d*) Enterprise resource programme

107. Identify the ERP vendor

(*a*) SAP (*b*) TCS (*c*) PATNI (*d*) CTS

108. SAP stands for

(*a*) System, Applications, Products in data processing
(*b*) Software, Applications, Products
(*c*) Software, Applications, Projects
(*d*) Software administration programme

109. How many layers are in the OSI reference model?

(*a*) 7 (*b*) 6 (*c*) 8 (*d*) 4

110. JAVA is a

(*a*) pure OOPS language (*b*) object based language
(*c*) script language (*d*) hypertext language

111. Scheduler in an operating system is

(*a*) an operating system module (*b*) a loader
(*c*) a compiler (*d*) a system call

112. Which of the following is used to convert a string to an integer?

(*a*) atoi() (*b*) itoa() (*c*) govt() (*d*) strcmp()

113. Which of the following returns a random number?

(*a*) rand( ) (*b*) random( ) (*c*) randomize( ) (*d*) r( )

114. The page fault frequency parameter 'p' is usually measured in

(*a*) number of page faults per millisecond (*b*) number of page faults per second
(*c*) number of page faults per minute (*d*) none of these

115. What are the two primitive operations of semaphore?

(*a*) SIGNAL & WAIT (*b*) BUSY & WAIT
(*c*) FREE & SIGNAL (*d*) WAIT & FREE

116. Name the operator which is automatically overloaded in JAVA.

(*a*) + (*b*) – (*c*) * (*d*) none of these

117. JAVA provides two different string classes from which string objects can be instantiated. What are they?

(*a*) String, StringBuffer (*b*) Strcmp, Strlen
(*c*) Strobj, String() (*d*) none of these

118. Which of the following is a keyword for handling exception in JAVA?

(*a*) try (*b*) static (*c*) obj (*d*) final

119. What method of which class would you use to extract the message from an exception object?

(*a*) The getMessage() method of the Throwable class
(*b*) The Message() method
(*c*) The GetMessage() method
(*d*) None of these

120. What is the name of the method that can be used to determine if a thread is alive?
(*a*) isAlive() (*b*) Alive() (*c*) islive() (*d*) none of these

121. Which of the following counts the number of current items in the list?
(*a*) Count (*b*) ListCount (*c*) CountList (*d*) none of these

122. The value returned by the MsgBox function when VbAbort is clicked is
(*a*) 1 (*b*) 2 (*c*) 3 (*d*) 4

123. StringBuffer class belongs to ....
(*a*) SDK (*b*) JDK (*c*) JAVA API (*d*) JVM

124. Which of the following creates a class that cannot be extended?
(*a*) abstract (*b*) final (*c*) public (*d*) all of these

125. Multithreading is implemented in JAVA through
(*a*) interface (*b*) class (*c*) methods (*d*) all of these

126. Which of the following statement can be used to come out of indefinite loops?
(*a*) break (*b*) switch (*c*) if (*d*) if-else

127. The character set of JAVA is called
(*a*) ASCII (*b*) BYTECODE (*c*) UNICODE (*d*) none of these

128. Which of the following in JAVA allows you to build GUI?
(*a*) SDK (*b*) AWT (*c*) JAVA BEANS (*d*) none of these

129. The extension for icon files is
(*a*) .icon (*b*) .ico (*c*) .ino (*d*) .inc

130. A function that does not return a value is called
(*a*) void (*b*) dynamic (*c*) static (*d*) constant

131. The method used to add items to the listbox control is
(*a*) AddListItem (*b*) AddItem (*c*) ListItem (*d*) AddList

132. In JAVA, Polymorphism is implemented by a technique called
(*a*) overloading (*b*) overriding (*c*) ADT (*d*) none of these

133. The three attributes that should be compulsorily used with <Applet> tags are
(*a*) Code, Name, Width (*b*) Name, Code, Height
(*c*) Code, Height (*d*) Name, Align

134. The method used to start the applets is
(*a*) Void start() (*b*) Start() (*c*) Void() (*d*) none of these

135. Multithreading is implemented in JAVA through an interface called
(*a*) Thread (*b*) Runnable (*c*) Start() (*d*) Init()

136. Which method is executed only once at the start of Applet execution?
(*a*) destroy() (*b*) start() (*c*) init() (*d*) stop()

137. The term 'bit' stands for

(*a*) byte digit (*b*) binary digit

(*c*) boolean digit (*d*) byte information transfer

138. Which one of the following is used for designing digital circuits in a digital computer?

(*a*) hardware (*b*) software

(*c*) boolean algebra (*d*) integrated circuit

139. Which one of the following is a combination of NOR gate?

(*a*) NOT & OR (*b*) NOT & AND

(*c*) AND & OR (*d*) AND, OR & NOT

140. Which one of the following is also called a flipflop?

(*a*) stable gate (*b*) logic stable gate (*c*) bi-stable gate (*d*) tri-stable gate

141. In which network, are computers connected to a central hub?

(*a*) star (*b*) bus (*c*) ring (*d*) hybrid

142. In which mode, can data be transmitted in one direction?

(*a*) simplex (*b*) half-duplex (*c*) full-duplex (*d*) a & b

143. Which one of the following is called ANSI standard of LINUX?

(*a*) shell (*b*) kernel (*c*) C language (*d*) none of these

144. In LINUX, which one of the following is the prompt for the root user?

(*a*) $ (*b*) @ (*c*) # (*d*) C

145. How many modes of operation are there in vi editor?

(*a*) 3 (*b*) 6 (*c*) 4 (*d*) 2

146. The boolean expression $\bar{A}\bar{B}\bar{C}+\bar{A}\bar{B}C+A\bar{B}\bar{C}+A\bar{B}C$ after simplification will be

(*a*) $\bar{B}$ (*b*) $\bar{A}$ (*c*) ABC (*d*) $\bar{A}\bar{B}\bar{C}$

147. Which one of the following establishes De-Morgan's first theorem?

(*a*) $A+B=\bar{A}.\bar{B}$ (*b*) $\overline{A+B}=\overline{A.B}$ (*c*) $\overline{A+B}=\bar{A}.\bar{B}$ (*d*) $\overline{A.B}=\bar{A}.\bar{B}$

148. Which of the following is an example of sequential circuit?

(*a*) flip-flop circuit (*b*) digital circuit

(*c*) logical circuit (*d*) combinational circuit

149. Which one of the following gates is called logical inverter?

(*a*) NAND (*b*) XOR (*c*) NOR (*d*) NOT

150. How many types of users are in the LINUX operating system?

(*a*) 2 (*b*) 3 (*c*) 4 (*d*) 6

151. Which one of the following is known as response time or latency?

(*a*) cycle time (*b*) memory time (*c*) access time (*d*) time

152. Which one of the following circuits is capable of storing one bit of information?

(*a*) full adder (*b*) half adder
(*c*) flip-flop (*d*) combinational circuit

153. How many stable states are there in a simple flip-flop?

(*a*) 5 (*b*) 2 (*c*) 3 (*d*) 4

154. Which command is used to show the contents of the file on the screen in LINUX?

(*a*) cat (*b*) man (*c*) pwd (*d*) echo

155. How many bytes of memory are required to store an integer?

(*a*) 8 (*b*) 2 (*c*) 4 (*d*) 1

156. The expression XYZ + XYZ + XYZ is called

(*a*) canonical sum (*b*) sum of standard product terms
(*c*) sum of minterms (*d*) all of these

157. DeMorgan's second theorem is

(*a*) $\overline{A.B} = \overline{A} + \overline{B}$ (*b*) $\overline{A.B} = \overline{A}.\overline{B}$ (*c*) A.B=A+B (*d*) $\overline{A}.\overline{B}$ =A+B

158. The device that accomplishes the modulation-demodulation process is called

(*a*) flip-flop (*b*) MODEM (*c*) chip (*d*) CPU

159. Job scheduling led to the concept known as the

(*a*) SPOOLING (*b*) resident monitors
(*c*) time-sharing (*d*) multiprogramming

160. Sending a message to a group is called

(*a*) multitasking (*b*) group message
(*c*) routing (*d*) multicast routing

161. An open source testing tool used to test the performance of the application when it is under heavy load is

(*a*) Apache JMeter (*b*) Loadrunner (*c*) TSL (*d*) PSP

162. The expected time to search for an element in a hash table is

(*a*) O(1) (*b*) O(2) (*c*) 0 (*d*) None of these

163. The Clique problem is

(*a*) NP-Complete (*b*) NP-Hard (*c*) NP-Soft (*d*) MST

164. The COCOMO model deals with

(*a*) software cost (*b*) software risk (*c*) scheduling (*d*) testing

165. What type of language is Visual Basic?

(*a*) object-based (*b*) object-oriented
(*c*) pure OOPS language (*d*) hypertext

166. The time complexity for Binary search algorithm is

(*a*) logn (*b*) O(logn) (*c*) O(1) (*d*) none of these

167. The mechanism by which two different file systems can be combined together is called

(*a*) mounting (*b*) paging (*c*) process (*d*) buddy system

168. A binary semaphore can take only one of the following 2 values:

(*a*) 0 and 1 (*b*) 0 and 10 (*c*) 0 and 2 (*d*) 1 and 10

169. What is the range of values ProcessID (PID) can take?

(*a*) 0 to 32767 (*b*) 0 to 128 (*c*) 0 to 256 (*d*) 0 to 1024

170. What is the system call to create a new process?

(*a*) fork (*b*) nice (*c*) exec( ) (*d*) brk( )

171. A Local variable which exists and retains its value even after the control is transferred to the calling function is called

(*a*) static variable (*b*) global variable
(*c*) temporary variable (*d*) constant variable

172. In header files, functions are

(*a*) declared (*b*) defined (*c*) called (*d*) overloaded

173. Which of the following allocates the requested size of bytes and returns a pointer to the first byte of the allocated space?

(*a*) malloc (*b*) calloc (*c*) realloc (*d*) none of these

174. Which of the following allocates space for an array of elements, initializes them to zero and then returns a pointer to the memory?

(*a*) malloc (*b*) calloc (*c*) realloc (*d*) none of these

175. Write down an equivalent pointer expression for referring to the same element a[i][j][k][l]

(*a*) *(*(*(*(a+i)+j)+k)+l) (*b*) a(*i+*j+*k+*l)
(*c*) *a[i][j][k][l] (*d*) a[*i][*j][*k][*l]

176. How will you declare an array of three function pointers where each function receives two integer values and returns a float?

(*a*) float (*arr[3](int,int); (*b*) float(arr[3](*int,*int);
(*c*) float (*arr[3])(&int,&int); (*d*) none of these.

177. How many bytes are occupied by the far, huge and near pointers?

(*a*) near pointer – 2 bytes, far and huge pointer – 4 bytes
(*b*) near pointer – 2 bytes, far and huge pointer – 2 bytes
(*c*) near pointer – 4 bytes, far and huge pointer – 4 bytes
(*d*) near pointer – 4 bytes, far and huge pointer – 2 bytes

178. The function atoi()

(*a*) converts a string to an integer (*b*) converts an integer to a string
(*c*) converts a floating point number to a string (*d*) none of these

179. The function itoa()

(*a*) converts a floating point number to a string
(*b*) converts an integer to a string
(*c*) converts a string to an integer
(*d*) none of these

180. The function govt()

(*a*) converts a string to an integer
(*b*) converts an integer to a string
(*c*) converts a floating point number to a string
(*d*) none of these

181. The rand() function returns a

(*a*) random number (*b*) 0 (*c*) –1 (*d*) garbage value

182. A Bus which carries the data to or from memory is known as a

(*a*) data bus (*b*) memory bus (*c*) I/O bus (*d*) none of these

183. Which of the following stores the result of each arithmetic or logical operation?

(*a*) accumulator (*b*) stack pointer (*c*) bus (*d*) CPU

184. A solution to the problem of indefinite blockage of low priority jobs is

(*a*) aging (*b*) simulation
(*c*) event-driven programs (*d*) none of these

185. The wasted bytes allocated to keep everything in units of blocks (instead of bytes) are called

(*a*) partition (*b*) external fragmentation
(*c*) internal fragmentation (*d*) deallocation

186. Name the technique of dividing each bit period into two equal intervals.

(*a*) manchester encoding (*b*) modulator
(*c*) transponders (*d*) multiplexer

187. Which of the following is used to control concurrent access of data between users?

(*a*) locks (*b*) forms (*c*) views (*d*) none of these

188. Name the database object which is used as an alternative name for a table, view or sequences. They are also used to simplify SQL statements.

(*a*) synonym (*b*) sequences (*c*) index (*d*) none of these

189. Name the database object which can generate unique, sequential integer values.

(*a*) sequence (*b*) synonym (*c*) view (*d*) index

190. Name a special bit pattern that circulates around the ring whenever all stations are idle.

(*a*) token (*b*) token ring (*c*) token bus (*d*) bridge

191. PAR stands for

(*a*) Positive acknowledgement with retransmission

(*b*) Program access registers

(*c*) Program address register

(*d*) Positive acknowledgement without retransmission

192. Which of the following deals with software cost estimation?

(*a*) COCOMO model (*b*) spiral model (*c*) prototyping model (*d*) RAD model

193. Name the software development approach that deals with risk prone projects and unstable requirements.

(*a*) extreme programming (*b*) system programming

(*c*) application programming (*d*) reengineering

194. When does software testing end?

(*a*) when we run out of time (*b*) when we run out of memory

(*c*) when there is no error (*d*) verification & validation are completed

195. Cyclomatic complexity is a software metric dealing with

(*a*) basis path testing (*b*) regression testing

(*c*) smoke testing (*d*) mutation testing

196. MTBF is equal to

(*a*) MTTF-MTTR (*b*) MTTR-MTTF

(*c*) MTTF*MTTR (*d*) MTTF-2*(MTTR)

197. Name the quality management technique that translates the needs of the customer into technical requirements.

(*a*) QFD (*b*) SRS (*c*) CSPEC (*d*) PSPEC

198. Which of the following is an OOPS metric?

(*a*) LOC (*b*) cyclomatic complexity

(*c*) NOC (*d*) comment %

199. Software configuration management deals with

(*a*) change management (*b*) requirements specification

(*c*) risk analysis (*d*) reengineering

200. How are the risks documented in SDLC?

(*a*) using RIS (*b*) using Risk Table (*c*) RMMM (*d*) KPA

201. A web server sends a program to be stored on the user's hard drive called a ....frequently without a disclosure or the user's content.

(*a*) cookie (*b*) website (*c*) server (*d*) datastore

202. The process of encrypting and decrypting messages is called................

(*a*) cryptography (*b*) authenticity

(*c*) cryptanalysis (*d*) authentication

203. A situation where a business is selling online to an individual consumer is

(*a*) Business-to-Consumer E-Commerce
(*b*) Business-to-Business E-Commerce
(*c*) E-Business
(*d*) banner

204. The processing time of a business process from beginning to end is

(*a*) cycle time
(*b*) lead time
(*c*) lapsed time
(*d*) process time

205. Computer-to-Computer direct transfer of standard business documents is

(*a*) EDI (Electronic data interchange)
(*b*) EFT (Electronic Fund transfer)
(*c*) Electronic distributor
(*d*) e-broker

206. A network that links the intranets of business partners using the virtually private network on the Internet is

(*a*) Extranet (*b*) Intranet (*c*) VAN (*d*) MAN

207. A network node consisting of both hardware and software that isolates a private network from public networks is

(*a*) firewall (*b*) fare tracker (*c*) intermediary (*d*) internet mall

208. The concept of delivering the ordered items at a designated time is

(*a*) JIT (Just-in-time)
(*b*) ontime shipping
(*c*) online delivery
(*d*) none of these

209. Which among the following is not a structured data type in C?

(*a*) union (*b*) pointer (*c*) string (*d*) boolean

210. A B-Tree of order m is an m-way search tree with

(*a*) all leaves of the tree on the same level
(*b*) each node, except for root and leaves, having less than m/2 subtrees
(*c*) the root of the tree having more than m subtrees
(*d*) all its leaves connected to form a linked list

211. A browser is a software tool that helps

(*a*) linking of application program modules
(*b*) viewing of application information
(*c*) developing application programs
(*d*) debugging of application software

212. Which of the following is not an element of C?

(*a*) tokens (*b*) identifiers (*c*) datatypes (*d*) structures

213. Which of the following is not an element of C++?

(*a*) tokens (*b*) identifiers (*c*) variables (*d*) constructors

214. Name the two communication satellites.

(*a*) geosynchronous and low-orbit
(*b*) synchronous and orbit
(*c*) geosynchronous and trunks
(*d*) trunks and tunneling

215. Which of the following is not a memory management scheme?

(*a*) paging memory (*b*) lock (*c*) mutual exclusion (*d*) critical region

216. Which of the following algorithm deals with deadlock?

(*a*) Banker's algorithm (*b*) Bakery algorithm
(*c*) RR (*d*) Priority algorithm

217. Which of the following is not an asymptotic notation?

(*a*) Big 'oh' (*b*) Omega (*c*) Theta (*d*) Alpha

218. Kuhn.-tucker conditions deal with

(*a*) non-linear programming (*b*) matroids
(*c*) LPP (*d*) assignment problem

219. The Max-Flow-Min-Cut theorem deals with

(*a*) network flow problem (*b*) LPP
(*c*) matroids (*d*) non-linear programming

220. Internet-based broadcasting of audio and video content is

(*a*) webcasting (*b*) webonomics
(*c*) webhosting (*d*) web content design

221. The placement of the website on a certain server and providing the necessary infrastructure for its operations is

(*a*) web hosting (*b*) webcasting (*c*) webonomics (*d*) webserver

222. Which of the following is CORRECT?

(*a*) Java does not support ICMP

(*b*) Java does not allow you to send raw IP packets

(*a*) (*a*) is true (*b*) (*b*) is true
(*c*) (*a*) and (*b*) are true (*d*) depends on data.

223. A typical C program is made up of several functions which may be contained in

(*a*) only one source file (*b*) one or more source files
(*c*) depends on functions (*d*) two or more source files

224. Every C program must have a

(*a*) main() (*b*) void main() (*c*) conio.h (*d*) getch()

225. In C, the semicolon is used as

(*a*) statement terminator (*b*) separator
(*c*) null statement (*d*) new line generator

226. A free tree is defined as a connected undirected graph with

(*a*) 1 cycle (*b*) 2 cycles (*c*) 3 cycles (*d*) no cycle

227. Depth-first traversal of a graph is roughly analogous to..........traversal

(*a*) preorder (*b*) inorder (*c*) level-by-level (*d*) postorder

228. The method of writing all operators either before their operands, or after them, is called

(*a*) polish notation (*b*) infix (*c*) postfix (*d*) prefix

229. A linked binary tree with n nodes, n>=0 has exactly............NULL links.

(*a*) n (*b*) n+1 (*c*) n–1 (*d*) n+2

230. A priority queue is a data structure with only two operations

(*a*) insert an item, remove an item having the largest or smallest key

(*b*) inserting and ordering the items

(*c*) removing and ordering the items

(*d*) inserting and setting priority value to existing items

231. The process of splitting a text or expression into pieces to determine its syntax is called

(*a*) parsing (*b*) recursive descent (*c*) pruning (*d*) token

232. The subscript of an array must be

(*a*) >0 (*b*) >1 (*c*) negative (*d*) >=0

233. Instance variables are the variables that are declared within a ....

(*a*) class (*b*) method (*c*) objects (*d*) constructor

234. The size of the applet viewer window can be determined by using the method

(*a*) getSize() (*b*) int getDescent

(*c*) int getHeight() (*d*) int getAscent

235. The process of removing errors from a program is called ....

(*a*) testing code (*b*) documentation (*c*) debugging (*d*) bug

236. How many characters are there in the ASCII characters set?

(*a*) 127 (*b*) 128 (*c*) 129 (*d*) 130

237. In Java, the index number of a string always starts with

(*a*) 0 (*b*) 1 (*c*) 2 (*d*) 3

238. Mnemonics are provided by

(*a*) algorithm (*b*) high level language

(*c*) assembly language (*d*) machine language

239. The subscript cannot be

(*a*) an integer (*b*) positive number (*c*) negative number (*d*) equal to 0

240. ....is a class modifier

(*a*) final (*b*) public (*c*) private (*d*) abstract

241. Which of the following is used to determine prime implicants and minimal forms for Boolean expressions?

(*a*) karnaugh map (*b*) truth table

(*c*) gate (*d*) inverter

242. Karnaugh map involves atmost..........variables

(*a*) 6 (*b*) 4 (*c*) 1 (*d*) 2

243. Which attribute is not compulsory with the applet tag?

(*a*) code base (*b*) height (*c*) width (*d*) code

244. The method which returns the current capacity of the stringbuffer object is

(*a*) capacity() (*b*) length() (*c*) buffercapacity() (*d*) capa()

245. Which one of the following is not a method included in java.applet.Applet class.............

(*a*) start() (*b*) stop() (*c*) destroy() (*d*) end()

246. Find out the super class of all applets.

(*a*) java.awt.graphics (*b*) java.applet.Applet

(*c*) java.applet (*d*) java.awt.*;

247. A function can return.................

(*a*) many values (*b*) two values (*c*) only one value (*d*) three values

248. Find the odd one out:

(*a*) class diagram (*b*) activity diagram (*c*) sequence diagram (*d*) DFD

249. In solving a problem, the sequence of steps to be carried out is called...........

(*a*) a program (*b*) a flow-chart (*c*) a pseudo code (*d*) an algorithm

250. Which of the following is INCORRECT?

(*a*) Validation takes place after verification

(*b*) Verification takes place after validation

(*a*) a (*b*) b

(*c*) depends on software (*d*) depends on data

251. The destructed object is ....and ....

(*a*) memory reclaimed and garbage collected (*b*) destroyed and thrown away

(*c*) reused and implemented (*d*) none of the above

252. When a subclass is derived from a single super class, the inheritance is called.........

(*a*) single inheritance (*b*) double inheritance

(*c*) multiple inheritance (*d*) none of the above

253. The ....keyword halts the execution of the current loop out of the loop

(*a*) continue (*b*) break

(*c*) sleep (*d*) none of the above

254. The AWT is a package of classes that helps in

(*a*) writing character based applications (*b*) creating GUI based applications

(*c*) creating networking applications (*d*) none of the above

255. A........defines the shape and behaviour of an object and is a template for multiple objects with similar features.

(*a*) Struct (*b*) Class

(*c*) template (*d*) none of the above

256. An EventListener interface defines one or more methods to be invoked by the

(*a*) Event source (*b*) Event listener

(*c*) Event class (*d*) none of the above.

257. The.......read b.length bytes into the array b and returns the actual number of bytes successfully read.

(*a*) read[] (*b*) read(byte[])

(*c*) read[byte b()] (*d*) none of the above

258. To import a class, the...........keyword should be used.

(*a*) new (*b*) import

(*c*) static (*d*) none of the above

259. The........is used to find the length of an array.

(*a*) Dot operator (*b*) Length

(*c*) new keyword (*d*) none of the above

260. An applet can also be executed using......application, which is a part of the JDK.

(*a*) Appletviewer (*b*) javac

(*c*) javacc (*d*) none of the above

261. The keyword...........is used to enable synchronization.

(*a*) runnable (*b*) synchronized

(*c*) throwable (*d*) none of the above

262. The most commonly used protocol of the web is

(*a*) SMTP (*b*) HTTP

(*c*) NNTP (*d*) none of the above

263. The......class is a non-abstract, recursively nestable container.

(*a*) button (*b*) panel

(*c*) list (*d*) none of the above

264. Each property is treated as........of the class.

(*a*) attribute (*b*) instance

(*c*) variable (*d*) none of the above

265. The.........keyword indicates that it is a class method and can be accessed without creating an object.

(*a*) static (*b*) local

(*c*) extern (*d*) none of the above

266. Two or more processes running concurrently in a computer is called............

(*a*) multithreading (*b*) multiprogramming
(*c*) multitasking (*d*) none of the above

267. ....are used to destroy the objects created using constructors.

(*a*) deletors (*b*) finalizers
(*c*) final (*d*) none of the above

268. ....method sets background color of the applet.

(*a*) Background() (*b*) setBackground()
(*c*) setbackground() (*d*) none of the above

269. The.......lays out components in a way very similar to a spreadsheet by rows and columns.

(*a*) Gridlayout (*b*) Flowlayout
(*c*) Borderlayout (*d*) none of the above

270. The.......method is used to print error messages.

(*a*) System.out (*b*) Syste.err
(*c*) System.error (*d*) none of the above

271. ....is a program that helps us log on to other networks.

(*a*) Usenet (*b*) Finger service
(*c*) FTP (*d*) none of the above

272. ....is a program or a tool that helps in locating a file anywhere on the net.

(*a*) FTP (*b*) Telnet
(*c*) Archie (*d*) none of the above

273. The default alignment of a line is..........

(*a*) low (*b*) bottom left
(*c*) bottom right (*d*) none of the above

274. A hyperlink can be............

(*a*) text only (*b*) image only
(*c*) text or image (*d*) none of the above

275. The tag used for comments in java is

(*a*) // (*b*) **
(*c*) /*....*/ (*d*) none of the above

276. The default method to submit data to the server is...........

(*a*) GET (*b*) POST (*c*) SEND (*d*) END

277. ....allows division of a document into distinct sections.

(*a*) buttons (*b*) panel
(*c*) grid (*d*) none of the above

278. The following datatypes are supported by the Javascript

(*a*) number only (*b*) strings only
(*c*) both Null and Boolean (*d*) none of the above

279. ....is used to define the name and properties of the object.

(*a*) destructor (*b*) #define
(*c*) constructor (*d*) none of the above

280. Parsing involves evaluating each line of the script code and converting it to.......

(*a*) an integer (*b*) a string
(*c*) bytes (*d*) pseudo-compiled byte code

281. Java is an......and ....language developed by Sun Microsystems in 1991.

(*a*) object-oriented, multi-threaded (*b*) object-oriented, multi-tasking
(*c*) structured and procedural (*d*) script and web design

282. The......class accepts input by using a buffered array of bytes that acts as cache.

(*a*) buffer (*b*) inputstream
(*c*) outputstream (*d*) none of the above

283. Networking in Java is possible through the use of

(*a*) Java.net (*b*) Java.networks
(*c*) Java.networking (*d*) none of the above

284. ....variables can be declared as final variables.

(*a*) temporary (*b*) auto
(*c*) global (*d*) none of the above

285. To find out what class the object belongs to, the......can be used.

(*a*) get() (*b*) Get()
(*c*) GetClass() (*d*) none of the above

286. ....is a 32 bit number which has four numbers separated by periods.

(*a*) IP address (*b*) URL (*c*) DNS (*d*) FTP

287. ....layout is often used along with panels to divide the screen space into number of cells.

(*a*) FlowLayout (*b*) GridLayout
(*c*) BorderLayout (*d*) none of the above

288. The object class has a subclass called...........to handle exceptions and errors.

(*a*) Throwable (*b*) ThrowEnabled
(*c*) Throwing (*d*) none of the above

289. Which two files are used during operation of the DBMS?

(*a*) SQL and PL/SQL (*b*) DML and query language
(*c*) Data dictionary and transaction log (*d*) Data dictionary and DDL.

290. A data dictionary is a special file that contains
(*a*) the names of all fields in all fields (*b*) the data types of all fields in all files
(*c*) the widths of all fields in all files (*d*) metadata

291. An information system that supplies information specifically to aid managers with decision-making responsibilities is called a
(*a*) DBMS (*b*) MIS (*c*) DSS (*d*) ERP

292. The longest sequence of events in a project is called the............path.
(*a*) critical path (*b*) activity path (*c*) complex path (*d*) PERT

293. PERT and CPM are...........techniques.
(*a*) network (*b*) assignment
(*c*) project evaluation (*d*) project management

294. Hungarian method is a way of solving operations research problem in
(*a*) LPP (*b*) simplex method
(*c*) assignment method (*d*) transportation method

295. A constraint that does not affect the feasible solution region is known as
(*a*) redundant constraint (*b*) slack variable
(*c*) surplus variable (*d*) optimality

296. Probability normally range from
(*a*) 0 to 1 (*b*) 0 to 0.1
(*c*) 1 to 100 (*d*) depends on the sample space

297. In compilers, the syntax analysis is done by
(*a*) lexical analyzer (*b*) syntax analyzer
(*c*) parser (*d*) code generator

298. Binary means........
(*a*) two (*b*) three (*c*) four (*d*) five

299. The hexadecimal digits are 0 to 9 and A to........
(*a*) D (*b*) E (*c*) F (*d*) Z

300. BCD numbers express each digit as a ....
(*a*) byte (*b*) nibble (*c*) bit (*d*) integer

301. An XOR gate recognizes only words with an..........number of 1's.
(*a*) odd (*b*) even
(*c*) depends on input (*d*) none of these

302. The EXCLUSIVE – NOR gate is equivalent to a........gate followed by an inverter.
(*a*) OR (*b*) AND (*c*) NAND (*d*) XOR

303. A shift register can be used for

(*a*) parallel to serial conversion (*b*) serial to parallel conversion
(*c*) digital delay line (*d*) all of these

304. ....is known as universal gate.

(*a*) NOT gate (*b*) NAND gate (*c*) OR gate (*d*) NOR gate

305. A multiplexer is also known as.........

(*a*) encoder (*b*) decoder
(*c*) data selector (*d*) data distributor

306. Which is the earliest and most widely used shell that came with the UNIX system?

(*a*) C shell (*b*) Korn shell (*c*) Bourne (*d*) Smith shell

307. A single character input from the keyboard can be obtained by using the function

(*a*) printf() (*b*) scanf() (*c*) getchar() (*d*) putchar()

308. What will be the output for the following?

```
#inlcude <stdio.h>
main()
{
float f;
f=10/3;
printf("%d",f);
}
```

(*a*) 3.3 (*b*) 3.0
(*c*) 3 (*d*) 3.33333333333

309. The function that sets the position to a desired point in the file is

(*a*) fseek() (*b*) ftell() (*c*) getw() (*d*) putc()

310. The process of calling a function using pointers to pass the address of variable is known as

(*a*) call by value (*b*) call by reference
(*c*) pointer argument (*d*) address value

311. Enumeration is

(*a*) a set of integers (*b*) a list of strings
(*c*) a set of legal values possible for a variable (*d*) a list of operators

312. The C language was developed by

(*a*) Marting Richards (*b*) Dennis Ritchie (*c*) Brain (*d*) Kanitkar

313. The comments in C language are placed between

(*a*) /* and *\ (*b*) /* and */ (*c*) //*and */ / (*d*) # and #

314. In C language, '5' represents
(*a*) an integer (*b*) a string
(*c*) a character (*d*) alphanumeral

315. goto is a...........in C programming language
(*a*) label (*b*) keyword (*c*) function (*d*) procedure

316. The statement printf("%5.4f", 1.23459); in C prints the following:
(*a*) 1.234560 (*b*) 1.2346 (*c*) 1.2345 (*d*) 1.234

317. The null character is represented by
(*a*) \n (*b*) \0 (*c*) \o (*d*) \t

318. The bitwise OR operator is a
(*a*) unary operator (*b*) binary operator
(*c*) digital operator (*d*) logical operator

319. Which programming language was used for writing the UNIX operating system?
(*a*) C (*b*) C++ (*c*) PASCAL (*d*) BASIC

320. In OSI network architecture, the routing is performed by
(*a*) network layer (*b*) transport layer (*c*) sessions layer (*d*) physical layer

321. A device that converts digital signals to analog signals is
(*a*) modem (*b*) demodulator (*c*) converter (*d*) simplifier

322. End-to-End connectivity is provided from host-to-host in.........
(*a*) transport layer (*b*) physical layer (*c*) router (*d*) hub

323. Which of the following deals with error detection at a data link layer?
(*a*) bit stuffing (*b*) hamming codes
(*c*) character stuffing (*d*) cyclic redundancy codes

324. A device that links two homogeneous packet-broadcast local networks is
(*a*) bridge (*b*) hub (*c*) router (*d*) repeater

325. Which of the following TCP/IP protocol is used for remote terminal connection service?
(*a*) TELNET (*b*) FTP (*c*) SLIP (*d*) TFTP

326. A MODEM is connected in between a telephone line and a
(*a*) computer (*b*) serial port (*c*) parallel port (*d*) adapter

327. Method of detecting and correcting transmission errors in data is known as
(*a*) handshake (*b*) debugging (*c*) hamming code (*d*) checksum

328. Which of the following is used to minimize data errors when data is transferred?
(*a*) checksum (*b*) check bit (*c*) transmit (*d*) patching

329. ALGOL is a............language.
(*a*) algorithmic (*b*) assembly (*c*) machine (*d*) low level

330. The symbols used in assembly language are

(*a*) codes (*b*) mnemonics (*c*) # (*d*) 0 and 1

331. The time required for the fetching and execution of one sample machine instruction is

(*a*) throughput (*b*) CPU cycle (*c*) access time (*d*) seek time

332. The range of frequencies available for data transmission is known as

(*a*) baud (*b*) bandwidth (*c*) byte (*d*) bits

333. The term MIPS refers to

(*a*) million instructions per second (*b*) million instructions per minute
(*c*) million information per second (*d*) megabytes of instruction per system

334. Banker's algorithm deals with

(*a*) deadlock avoidance (*b*) deadlock prevention
(*c*) critical region (*d*) segmentation

335. The term 'process' in operating system refers to

(*a*) program in execution (*b*) sequence of events
(*c*) set of jobs (*d*) segments

336. The Round Robin scheduling is essentially the preemptive version of

(*a*) FIFO (*b*) LIFO (*c*) SJF (*d*) SSTE

337. The principal of 'locality of reference' justifies the use of

(*a*) cache memory (*b*) virtual memory
(*c*) paging (*d*) segmentation

338. CAD/CAM is the inter-relationship between

(*a*) design and manufacturing
(*b*) design and marketing
(*c*) design and management
(*d*) engineering and materials management

339. Name the register or storage location that forms the result of arithmetic or logic operation?

(*a*) accumulator (*b*) adapter (*c*) memory registers (*d*) processor

340. Name the interface card that allows the PC to connect to peripheral?

(*a*) adapter (*b*) MODEM (*c*) connector (*d*) cell

341. Name the device which regenerates an analogue signal, thus increasing the distance with which the signal can be sent?

(*a*) amplifier (*b*) regulator
(*c*) multiplexer (*d*) analog transmitter

342. Which of the following is used to change the shape of an object?

(*a*) aspect ratio (*b*) assembler (*c*) attenuation (*d*) appletalk

343. Name the electronic tube with a screen upon which information may be displayed?

(*a*) carrier (*b*) screen (*c*) monitor (*d*) CRT

343. The provision of a direct, dedicated, physical path between two communicating devices is referred as

(*a*) circuit switching (*b*) packet switching (*c*) diode (*d*) cabling

344. The degree of dependence of one module upon another is called

(*a*) coupling (*b*) cohesion (*c*) data independence (*d*) modularity

345. The simultaneous sending and receiving of data over a communication path is called

(*a*) full-duplex transmission (*b*) simplex transmission
(*c*) half-duplex transmission (*d*) full-duplex frame

346. Name the bar chart that depicts the timing of completion of a series of tasks?

(*a*) pie chart (*b*) gantt chart (*c*) histogram (*d*) PERT

347. The fetch and decode steps in the process of performing an instruction is called

(*a*) instruction cycle (*b*) instruction set (*c*) process cycle (*d*) instructor

348. Internet is a

(*a*) VAN (*b*) set of computers
(*c*) network of network (*d*) collection of routers

349. Which of the following is not a memory management technique?

(*a*) paging (*b*) segmentation (*c*) demand paging (*d*) thrashing

350. Which of the following is related with operating system?

(*a*) CRT (*b*) SPOOL (*c*) multiplexing (*d*) crashing

351. ....is a declaration of a function type (what it returns) and the number and type of arguments, if any, that the function expects.

(*a*) function prototype (*b*) function call
(*c*) function declaration (*d*) function definition

352. The information we pass to the function is called..........

(*a*) argument (*b*) reference
(*c*) parameter (*d*) function prototype

353. An element of a structure can be a pointer to another structure of the same type. This is called a ....

(*a*) class (*b*) nested structures
(*c*) self-referential structure (*d*) pointer to structure

354. Which of the following is not a reserved word in C?

(*a*) for (*b*) goto (*c*) if (*d*) newline

355. Which of the following is used when dereferencing a pointer to a structure?

(*a*) arrow operator (*b*) dot operator
(*c*) & (*d*) member name as declared in structure

356. Which of the following is not a network topology?

(*a*) star (*b*) ring (*c*) mesh (*d*) square

357. A forest 'F' is a set of

(*a*) rooted trees (*b*) nodes (*c*) B-tree (*d*) set of subtrees

358. An orchard 'O' will consist of

(*a*) an ordered tree (*b*) B-tree (*c*) subtree (*d*) rooted tree

359. A free tree is defined as a connected undirected graph with

(*a*) two cycles (*b*) only one cycle (*c*) no cycles (*d*) three cycles

360. All internal nodes except the root have at most 'm' children, and at least %m/2% children is the property of

(*a*) B-Tree (*b*) forest
(*c*) AVL tree (*d*) binary search tree

361. Translation of an expression by recursive descent is called......................

(*a*) parsing (*b*) top-down parsing
(*c*) pruning (*d*) polish notation

362. If E is a properly formed expression in postfix form, then E must satisfy the following condition.............

(*a*) race condition (*b*) running-sum condition
(*c*) quadratic formula (*d*) polish notation

363. A tree with n vertices is an __________ if each edge is assigned a unique positive integer between 1 and (n-1).

(*a*) edge-labeled tree (*b*) tree (*c*) rooted tree (*d*) AVL tree

364. Every branch of a spanning tree defines a ____________

(*a*) unique fundamental cut-set (*b*) cut-set
(*c*) cut-vertex (*d*) tree

365. In order to traverse a graph we have to process every node exactly __________.

(*a*) once (*b*) twice (*c*) thrice (*d*) at least twice

366. Generally two traversal techniques are used for the graph____________.

(*a*) depth-first search, breadth-first search (*b*) top down and bottom up
(*c*) greedy and dynamic strategy (*d*) depth and best-first search

367. The Breath-first search maintains a ________, first-in, first-out where the unvisited elements are kept.

(*a*) stack (*b*) queue (*c*) linked list (*d*) list

368. The predecessor pointers of the breadth-first search defines __________

(*a*) tree (*b*) inverted tree (*c*) stack (*d*) queue

369. Whenever depth-first search applies on any graph, it yields a ________.

(*a*) tree (*b*) depth-first tree
(*c*) list (*d*) best-first search

370. Let a graph G = (V,E), if 'T' is a sub-graph of G and contains all the vertices but no cycle circuit, then 'T' is said to be a ______.

(*a*) tree (*b*) spanning tree (*c*) cycle (*d*) AVL tree

371. A minimum spanning tree (MST in short) is a spanning tree of ________.

(*a*) no weight (*b*) minimum weight (*c*) large weight (*d*) none of these

372. For computing the minimum cost spanning tree there are two algorithms ________ which are based on greedy technique.

(*a*) breadth-first and depth-first (*b*) Kruskal's and Prim's
(*c*) breadth-first and best-first (*c*) Kruskal's and Dynamic programming

373. The ________ is based upon dynamic programming technique in which the key part is to reduce a large problem into smaller problems.

(*a*) heuristic algorithm (*b*) floyd-warshall algorithm
(*c*) MST (*d*) graphs

374. A ______ is a weighted graph or a weighted digraph.

(*a*) MST (*b*) network (*c*) connected graph (*d*) cut-set

375. A ________ is a digraph whose underlying graph is a forest

(*a*) tree (*b*) directed forest (*c*) MST (*d*) inverted tree

376. If a graph is strongly connected, it has an arborescence rooted at ________

(*a*) every edge (*b*) every vertex (*c*) every tree (*d*) any vertex

377. The number of fundamental cycles of a connected graph with respect to a spanning tree is ________

(*a*) 0 (*b*) based on vertices & edges
(*c*) 1 (*d*) none of these

378. Network – flow problems can be formulated and solved using ______

(*a*) tree (*b*) MST (*c*) graphs (*d*) None of these

379. The max-flow min-cut theorem is related to

(*a*) IC (*b*) OR (*c*) graphs (*d*) stack

380. A project is divided into many well-defined and non overlapping individual jobs, called ________

(*a*) events (*b*) path (*c*) activities (*d*) subnet

381. A ______ can be drawn to depict the project

(*a*) graph (*b*) tree (*c*) weighted graph (*d*) PERT

382. A weighted, connected digraph representing activities in a project is called an ________

(*a*) forest (*b*) CPM (*c*) activity network (*d*) network

383. The vertex denoting the termination of the project must have ________

(*a*) zero in-degree (*b*) null vertex (*c*) zero out-degree (*d*) null tree

384. The longest directed path is called a ________.

(*a*) path (*b*) longest path (*c*) critical path (*d*) directed graph

385. ________ is white-box testing technique first proposed by Tom McCabe.

(*a*) flow graphs (*b*) decision tree (*c*) basis path testing (*d*) smoke testing

386. A flowchart is used to depict ________

(*a*) switch statement (*b*) structure
(*c*) class (*d*) program control structure

387. ________ is software metric that provides a quantitative measure of the logic complexity of a program.

(*a*) WMC (*b*) LOC
(*c*) DIT (*d*) cyclomatic complexity

388. Cyclomatic complexity, V(G), for a flow graph, G, is defined as ________.
(N- Number of vertices and E- Number of edges)

(*a*) V(G) = E+N+2 (*b*) V(G) = E–N–2
(*c*) V(G) = E*N+2 (*d*) V(G) = E–N+2

389. The basis path testing method can be applied to a ________

(*a*) source code only (*b*) structure
(*c*) class (*d*) procedural design or source code

390. To develop a software tool that assists in basis path testing, a data structure called a ________, can be quite useful.

(*a*) stack (*b*) queue (*c*) linked list (*d*) graph matrix

391. ________ can also be applied at the behavioral (black-box) level. The graph will assist in identifying those loops that need to be tested.

(*a*) control testing (*b*) smoke testing (*c*) regression testing (*d*) loop testing

392. ________________helps in analyzing the intrinsic parallelism of a program.

(*a*) decision table (*b*) decision tree
(*c*) DFD (*d*) structured chart

393. Which of the following is not a part of SDLC?

(*a*) analysis (*b*) software cost estimation
(*c*) design (*d*) SRS

394. Which of the following is not a part of software testing?

(*a*) fixing bugs (*b*) debugging (*c*) V&V (*d*) fault tolerance

395. .... is an umbrella activity that is applied throughout the software process.

(*a*) SQA (*b*) V&V
(*c*) configuration management (*d*) change management

396. FTR (Formal technical review) is a ....performed by software engineers.

(*a*) software quality assurance activity (*b*) software testing activity
(*c*) change management activity (*d*) configuration management activity

397. Which of the following addresses both software and hardware quality management?

(*a*) CMM (*b*) PCMM (*c*) TQM (*d*) CMMI

398. How many classes of loops are there?

(*a*) 1 (*b*) 2 (*c*) 3 (*d*) 4

399. Which of the following is an approach of integration testing?

(*a*) stress testing (*b*) performance testing
(*c*) smoke testing (*d*) V&V

400. Which of the following testing tool is used to test client/server applications?

(*a*) JMeter (*b*) Load Runner (*c*) Win Runner (*d*) TSL

401. .... is an informal meeting for evaluation or informational purposes?

(*a*) inspection (*b*) walkthrough (*c*) review (*d*) testing

402. ....is a document that describes the objectives, scope, approach, and focus of a software testing effort.

(*a*) software test case (*b*) software test plan
(*c*) TSL (*d*) test design

403. A .... is a document that describes an input, action, or event and an expected response, to determine if a feature of an application is working correctly.

(*a*) test document (*b*) test case (*c*) test plan (*d*) test file

404. What to do when there is no enough time for thorough testing?

(*a*) use risk analysis (*b*) use SCM
(*c*) use test budget (*d*) reduce test cases

405. Which of the following can be quite complex to test?

(*a*) open systems (*b*) OOPS
(*c*) packaged software (*d*) C/S application

406. ....software metric deals with counting all physical lines of code, the number of statements and the number comment lines.

(*a*) line count (*b*) CC (*c*) WMC (*d*) DIT

407. .... is a count of the methods implemented within a class or the sum of the complexities of the methods.

(*a*) weighted methods per class (*b*) DIT
(*c*) CC (*d*) NOC

408. .... is the cardinality of the set of all methods that can be invoked in response to a message to an object of the class or by some method in the class.

(*a*) response for a class (*b*) weighted methods per class
(*c*) mapping cardinality (*d*) cardinality ratio

409. High cohesion indicates ....

(*a*) good class subdivision (*b*) poor class subdivision
(*c*) complexity of a class (*d*) reliability of a software module

410. .... is a count of the number of other classes to which a class is coupled.

(*a*) coupling between object classes (CBO) (*b*) DIT
(*c*) LCOM (*d*) cyclomatic complexity

411. ....is the number of immediate subclasses subordinate to a class in the hierarchy.

(*a*) number of children (NOC) (*b*) LCOM
(*c*) coupling between object classes (CBO) (*d*) RFC

412. Which one of the following is related to recursion?

(*a*) stack (*b*) queue (*c*) linked list (*d*) tree

413. The insertion operation in a queue is called

(*a*) enqueue (*b*) dequeue (*c*) inqueue (*d*) insert

414. The deletion operation in a queue is called

(*a*) dequeue (*b*) enqueue (*c*) delete (*d*) delqueue

415. In a tree, nodes having degree zero are known as ....and the nodes other than these nodes are known as ....

(*a*) terminal nodes and non-terminal nodes (*b*) non-terminal nodes and terminal nodes
(*c*) root and leaf (*d*) leaf and root

416. The ....of a node are all the nodes along the path from the root node to that node.

(*a*) ancestors (*b*) path (*c*) depth (*d*) height

417. The ....of a tree is the maximum level of any node in the tree.

(*a*) height (*b*) weight (*c*) depth (*d*) length

418. ....is a special class of data structure in which the number of children of any node is restricted to atmost two.

(*a*) binary tree (*b*) heap (*c*) sparse matrix (*d*) AVL tree

419. A tree having 'm' nodes has exactly ....edges or branches.

(*a*) (m-1) (*b*) (m+1) (*c*) (m-2) (*d*) (m+2)

420. A tree is a ....

(*a*) non-linear data structure (*b*) linear data structure
(*c*) circular data structure (*d*) rooted structure

421. A.................is an ordered set of elements which is defined recursively.

(*a*) binomial tree (*b*) binomial heap
(*c*) fibonacci heap (*d*) binary tree

422. The running time for insertion sort algorithm under best case is

(*a*) O(n) (*b*) O(log n) (*c*) O(log n*n) (*d*) O(n log n)

423. The running time for merge sort algorithm under best case is

(*a*) O(n) (*b*) O(log n) (*c*) O(log n*n) (*d*) O(n log n)

424. Which of the following was introduced by Adelson-Velskii and Landis in 1962?

(*a*) AVL tree (*b*) binary tree (*c*) binary search tree (*d*) balanced tree

425. Which of the following reflects the balance factor for a node in AVL tree?

(*a*) {0,1,2} (*b*) {0,-1,1} (*c*) {0,1} (*d*) {-1,0,1}

426. Which of the following is not a property of Red-Black tree?

(*a*) the root node is coloured black
(*b*) the root node contains a value
(*c*) a red coloured node has no red coloured children
(*d*) every leaf node is coloured black

427. An edge to a black node in Red-Black tree is called

(*a*) red edge (*b*) black edge (*c*) black level (*d*) edge point

428. .... provides the direct access of record from the file no matter where the record is in the file.

(*a*) hashing (*b*) chaining (*c*) red-black tree (*d*) AVL tree

429. Which of the following deals with minimising collision?

(*a*) open addressing (*b*) closed addressing (*c*) sorting (*d*) linear probing

430. In Binary search tree, every node's value is greater than its ......and lesser than its ....

(*a*) left subtree, right subtree (*b*) right subtree, left subtree
(*c*) depends on root's value (*d*) depends on height of the tree

431. If any NP-complete problems belong to class P, then

(*a*) P=NP (*b*) P≥NP (*c*) P>NP (*d*) P<NP

432. Which of the following is true with respect to circular linked list?

(*a*) Last node points to the first node
(*b*) Last node contains null pointer
(*c*) If last node contains value, then it will not point to first node
(*d*) The first node and last node must contain the same value

433. The basic tree traversal techniques are

(*a*) breadth-first, depth-first and best-first (*b*) prefix, infix and postfix
(*c*) pre-order, in-order and post-order (*d*) breadth-first, depth-first and heuristic

434. The amount of time needed by an algorithm to run to completion is referred as

(*a*) space complexity (*b*) time complexity
(*c*) algorithm validation (*d*) execution time

435. An incorrect step, process, or data definition in a computer program is termed as

(*a*) fault (*b*) error (*c*) failure (*d*) None of these

436. To detect, locate, and correct faults in a computer program is called

(*a*) testing (*b*) debugging (*c*) error fixing (*d*) fault tolerance

437. Which of the following adversely affects software testing?

(*a*) poor project scheduling (*b*) unstable requirements
(*c*) complexity in design (*d*) LOC is high

438. Can we write a function similar to printf()?

(*a*) YES (*b*) NO
(*c*) depends on scanf() (*d*) using pointers only

439. Name the function which can be used to convert an integer or a float to a string?

(*a*) malloc() (*b*) sprintf() (*c*) typecasting (*d*) string()

440. What are the different file extensions that are created by Oracle Reports?

(*a*) .RDF file & .RPX file (*b*) .RDX file & .RDF file
(*c*) .REP file & .RDF file (*d*) none of these

441. SHOW_ALERT function returns

(*a*) boolean (*b*) number
(*c*) character (*d*) none of the above

442. What are the different events in Triggers?

(*a*) Define, Create (*b*) Drop, Comment
(*c*) Insert, Update, Delete (*d*) Update, Delete

443. Which of the following is VALID in PL/SQL ?

(*a*) Select ... into (*b*) Updates (*c*) Create (*d*) Deletes

444. Which of the following is CORRECT about Cursor?

(*a*) Cursor is a named PL/SQL area
(*b*) Cursor cannot holds results from a query
(*c*) Cursor is used for retrieving multiple rows
(*d*) SQL uses implicit Cursors to insert rows

445. Find the ODD one out?

(*a*) DDL (*b*) DML (*c*) DCL (*d*) PL/SQL

446. Which of the following is not correct about User_Defined Exceptions ?

(*a*) must be declared
(*b*) must be raised explicitly
(*c*) raised automatically in response to an oracle error
(*d*) none of these

447. Name the two parts of the procedure in ORACLE?

(*a*) procedure specification and procedure body.
(*b*) procedure definition and procedure body.
(*c*) procedure declaration and procedure body.
(*d*) none of these

448. Name the error handling part of PL/SQL block?

(*a*) exception (*b*) bug (*c*) trigger (*d*) debugging

449. Name the two types of cursors in PL/SQL?

(*a*) implicit and explicit cursors (*b*) internal and external cursors
(*c*) lower and higher level cursors (*d*) user defined and built-in cursors

450. In PL/SQL, the term PL stands for

(*a*) procedural language (*b*) programming language
(*c*) procedural latex (*d*) packaged language

ANSWERS

1. (*c*)	**44.** (*c*)	**87.** (*a*)	**130.** (*a*)	**173.** (*a*)	**216.** (*a*)
2. (*b*)	**45.** (*d*)	**88.** (*a*)	**131.** (*b*)	**174.** (*a*)	**217.** (*d*)
3. (*b*)	**46.** (*d*)	**89.** (*d*)	**132.** (*a*)	**175.** (*a*)	**218.** (*a*)
4. (*c*)	**47.** (*a*)	**90.** (*d*)	**133.** (*c*)	**176.** (*a*)	**219.** (*a*)
5. (*a*)	**48.** (*d*)	**91.** (*a*)	**134.** (*d*)	**177.** (*a*)	**220.** (*a*)
6. (*a*)	**49.** (*c*)	**92.** (*c*)	**135.** (*b*)	**178.** (*a*)	**221.** (*a*)
7. (*a*)	**50.** (*c*)	**93.** (*c*)	**136.** (*c*)	**179.** (*b*)	**222.** (*c*)
8. (*a*)	**51.** (*c*)	**94.** (*c*)	**137.** (*b*)	**180.** (*a*)	**223.** (*b*)
9. (*a*)	**52.** (*c*)	**95.** (*b*)	**138.** (*c*)	**181.** (*a*)	**224.** (*a*)
10. (*b*)	**53.** (*b*)	**96.** (*c*)	**139.** (*a*)	**182.** (*a*)	**225.** (*a*)
11. (*a*)	**54.** (*c*)	**97.** (*b*)	**140.** (*c*)	**183.** (*a*)	**226.** (*a*)
12. (*d*)	**55.** (*d*)	**98.** (*c*)	**141.** (*a*)	**184.** (*a*)	**227.** (*d*)
13. (*d*)	**56.** (*a*)	**99.** (*b*)	**142.** (*a*)	**185.** (*a*)	**228.** (*a*)
14. (*b*)	**57.** (*b*)	**100.** (*d*)	**143.** (*d*)	**186.** (*a*)	**229.** (*a*)
15. (*b*)	**58.** (*c*)	**101.** (*a*)	**144.** (*a*)	**187.** (*a*)	**230.** (*b*)
16. (*a*)	**59.** (*c*)	**102.** (*b*)	**145.** (*d*)	**188.** (*a*)	**231.** (*a*)
17. (*a*)	**60.** (*b*)	**103.** (*d*)	**146.** (*d*)	**189.** (*a*)	**232.** (*a*)
18. (*d*)	**61.** (*d*)	**104.** (*a*)	**147.** (*b*)	**190.** (*a*)	**233.** (*d*)
19. (*d*)	**62.** (*b*)	**105.** (*a*)	**148.** (*a*)	**191.** (*a*)	**234.** (*a*)
20. (*b*)	**63.** (*c*)	**106.** (*a*)	**149.** (*d*)	**192.** (*a*)	**235.** (*c*)
21. (*b*)	**64.** (*c*)	**107.** (*a*)	**150.** (*c*)	**193.** (*a*)	**236.** (*b*)
22. (*d*)	**65.** (*c*)	**108.** (*a*)	**151.** (*c*)	**194.** (*d*)	**237.** (*a*)
23. (*b*)	**66.** (*d*)	**109.** (*a*)	**152.** (*d*)	**195.** (*a*)	**238.** (*c*)
24. (*b*)	**67.** (*c*)	**110.** (*a*)	**153.** (*b*)	**196.** (*a*)	**239.** (*c*)
25. (*b*)	**68.** (*d*)	**111.** (*a*)	**154.** (*a*)	**197.** (*a*)	**240.** (*d*)
26. (*a*)	**69.** (*c*)	**112.** (*a*)	**155.** (*b*)	**198.** (*c*)	**241.** (*a*)
27. (*a*)	**70.** (*c*)	**113.** (*a*)	**156.** (*a*)	**199.** (*a*)	**242.** (*a*)
28. (*a*)	**71.** (*a*)	**114.** (*a*)	**157.** (*a*)	**200.** (*a*)	**243.** (*a*)
29. (*a*)	**72.** (*b*)	**115.** (*a*)	**158.** (*b*)	**201.** (*a*)	**244.** (*a*)
30. (*c*)	**73.** (*a*)	**116.** (*a*)	**159.** (*c*)	**202.** (*a*)	**245.** (*d*)
31. (*a*)	**74.** (*d*)	**117.** (*a*)	**160.** (*a*)	**203.** (*a*)	**246.** (*b*)
32. (*a*)	**75.** (*b*)	**118.** (*a*)	**161.** (*b*)	**204.** (*a*)	**247.** (*c*)
33. (*b*)	**76.** (*d*)	**119.** (*a*)	**162.** (*d*)	**205.** (*a*)	**248.** (*d*)
34. (*a*)	**77.** (*a*)	**120.** (*a*)	**163.** (*a*)	**206.** (*a*)	**249.** (*d*)
35. (*b*)	**78.** (*b*)	**121.** (*d*)	**164.** (*a*)	**207.** (*a*)	**250.** (*b*)
36. (*a*)	**79.** (*a*)	**122.** (*a*)	**165.** (*a*)	**208.** (*b*)	**251.** (*a*)
37. (*a*)	**80.** (*c*)	**123.** (*b*)	**166.** (*d*)	**209.** (*d*)	**252.** (*a*)
38. (*d*)	**81.** (*d*)	**124.** (*a*)	**167.** (*d*)	**210.** (*a*)	**253.** (*b*)
39. (*a*)	**82.** (*c*)	**125.** (*a*)	**168.** (*a*)	**211.** (*b*)	**254.** (*b*)
40. (*a*)	**83.** (*c*)	**126.** (*a*)	**169.** (*c*)	**212.** (*d*)	**255.** (*b*)
41. (*a*)	**84.** (*b*)	**127.** (*b*)	**170.** (*c*)	**213.** (*d*)	**256.** (*c*)
42. (*a*)	**85.** (*c*)	**128.** (*b*)	**171.** (*a*)	**214.** (*a*)	**257.** (*d*)
43. (*a*)	**86.** (*a*)	**129.** (*b*)	**172.** (*b*)	**215.** (*a*)	**258.** (*a*)

259. (*b*)	302. (*d*)	345. (*a*)	388. (*d*)	431. (*a*)
260. (*a*)	303. (*d*)	346. (*b*)	389. (*d*)	432. (*a*)
261. (*b*)	304. (*b*)	347. (*a*)	390. (*d*)	433. (*c*)
262. (*b*)	305. (*c*)	348. (*c*)	391. (*d*)	434. (*b*)
263. (*b*)	306. (*c*)	349. (*d*)	392. (*d*)	435. (*a*)
264. (*a*)	307. (*c*)	350. (*b*)	393. (*b*)	436. (*b*)
265. (*a*)	308. (*b*)	351. (*a*)	394. (*d*)	437. (*b*)
266. (*b*)	309. (*a*)	352. (*a*)	395. (*a*)	438. (*a*)
267. (*d*)	310. (*b*)	353. (*c*)	396. (*a*)	439. (*b*)
268. (*b*)	311. (*c*)	354. (*d*)	397. (*c*)	440. (*c*)
269. (*a*)	312. (*b*)	355. (*a*)	398. (*a*)	441. (*b*)
270. (*c*)	313. (*b*)	356. (*d*)	399. (*d*)	442. (*c*)
271. (*d*)	314. (*c*)	357. (*a*)	400. (*c*)	443. (*a*)
272. (*a*)	315. (*b*)	358. (*a*)	401. (*b*)	444. (*c*)
273. (*d*)	316. (*b*)	359. (*c*)	402. (*b*)	445. (*d*)
274. (*c*)	317. (*b*)	360. (*a*)	403. (*b*)	446. (*c*)
275. (*b*)	318. (*b*)	361. (*b*)	404. (*a*)	447. (*a*)
276. (*b*)	319. (*a*)	362. (*b*)	405. (*d*)	448. (*a*)
277. (*d*)	320. (*a*)	363. (*a*)	406. (*a*)	449. (*a*)
278. (*d*)	321. (*a*)	364. (*a*)	407. (*a*)	450. (*a*)
279. (*b*)	322. (*a*)	365. (*a*)	408. (*b*)	
280. (*b*)	323. (*d*)	366. (*a*)	409. (*a*)	
281. (*a*)	324. (*a*)	367. (*b*)	410. (*a*)	
282. (*d*)	325. (*a*)	368. (*b*)	411. (*a*)	
283. (*a*)	326. (*a*)	369. (*b*)	412. (*a*)	
284. (*d*)	327. (*c*)	370. (*b*)	413. (*a*)	
285. (*d*)	328. (*a*)	371. (*b*)	414. (*a*)	
286. (*a*)	329. (*a*)	372. (*b*)	415. (*a*)	
287. (*b*)	330. (*b*)	373. (*b*)	416. (*a*)	
288. (*a*)	331. (*b*)	374. (*b*)	417. (*a*)	
289. (*c*)	332. (*b*)	375. (*b*)	418. (*a*)	
290. (*d*)	333. (*a*)	376. (*b*)	419. (*a*)	
291. (*b*)	334. (*a*)	377. (*b*)	420. (*a*)	
292. (*a*)	335. (*a*)	378. (*c*)	421. (*a*)	
293. (*c*)	336. (*a*)	379. (*c*)	422. (*a*)	
294. (*c*)	337. (*a*)	380. (*c*)	423. (*d*)	
295. (*a*)	338. (*a*)	381. (*c*)	424. (*a*)	
296. (*a*)	339. (*a*)	382. (*c*)	425. (*d*)	
297. (*c*)	340. (*a*)	383. (*c*)	426. (*b*)	
298. (*a*)	341. (*a*)	384. (*c*)	427. (*b*)	
299. (*c*)	342. (*a*)	385. (*d*)	428. (*a*)	
300. (*b*)	343. (*d*)	386. (*d*)	429. (*d*)	
301. (*a*)	344. (*a*)	387. (*d*)	430. (*a*)	

Bibliography

1. "Understanding Pointers in C", Yashvant P. Kanetkar, BPB Publications, 1995.
2. "C – A Software Engineering Approach", Peter A. Darnell, Philip E. Margolis, Narosa Publishing House, 1991.
3. "Programming in ANSI C", E. Balagurusamy, Tata McGraw-Hill, 1998.
4. "Test Your C Skills", Yashvant P.Kanetkar, BPB Publications, 1996.
5. "Test your C++ skills", Yashvant P. Kanetkar, BPB Publications, 2002.
6. "Object-Oriented Programming in Turbo C++", Robert Lafore, Galgotia Publications, 1998.
7. "Software Enginnering", Roger S. Pressman, Tata McGraw-Hill, 2001.
8. "Software Testing Tools", Dr. K.V.K.K. Prasad, Dreamtech, NewDelhi, 2004.
9. "Enterprise Resource Planning", Alexis Leon, Tata McGraw-Hill, 2003.
10. "Introduction to Algorithms", Thomas H. Cormen, Prentice Hall of India, 2002.
11. "Java 2: The Complete Reference", Herbert Schildt, Tata McGraw-Hill, 2002.
12. "Operating System Concepts", Abraham Silberschatz, John Wiley & Sons, 2004.
13. "Digital Principles and Applications"; Albert Paul Malvino, Donald P. Leach, Tata McGraw-Hill, 1996.
14. "Database System Concepts", Abraham Silbertschatz, Henry F. Korth, S. Sudharshan, Tata McGraw-Hill, 1997.
15. "Computer Networks", Andrew S. Tenanbaum, Prentice Hall of India, 1997
16. "C Programming Language", Brain W. Kernighan and Dennis M.Ritchie, Prentice Hall of India, 1995.
17. "An Introduction to Database Systems", Date C.J., Addison Wesley Publishing Company, 1997.
18. "Electronic Commerce – A Managerial Perspective", Efraim Turban, Jae Lee, David King, H. Michael Chung, Pearson Education, 2000.
19. "Data Structures and Program Design in C", Robert L. Kruse, Bruce P. Leung, Clovis L. Tondo, Prentice Hall of India, 1998.